Fighting in Flan

By

E. Alexander Powell

Special Correspondent of The New York World
With The Belgian Forces In The Field

Author of "The Last Frontier"
"Gentlemen Ravers,"
"The End of the Trail,"
"The Road to Glory," etc.

With Illustrations from Photographs
By Mr. Donald Thompson

British Library Cataloguing-in-Publication Data
A catalogue record for this book is available from the
British Library

CONTENTS

THE CAMP FIRE GIRLS BEHIND THE LINES

Introduction to the

World War One Centenary Series

The First World War was a global war centred in Europe that began on 28 July 1914 and lasted until 11 November 1918. More than nine million combatants were killed, a casualty rate exacerbated by the belligerents' technological and industrial sophistication – and tactical stalemate. It was one of the deadliest conflicts in history, paving the way for major political changes, including revolutions in many of the nations involved. The war drew in all the world's great economic powers, which were assembled in two opposing alliances: the Allies (based on the Triple Entente of the United Kingdom, France and the Russian Empire) and the Central Powers of Germany and Austria-Hungary. These alliances were both reorganised and expanded as more nations entered the war: Italy, Japan and the United States joined the Allies, and the Ottoman Empire and Bulgaria joined the Central Powers. Ultimately, more than 70 million military personnel were mobilised.

The war was triggered by the assassination of Archduke Franz Ferdinand of Austria, heir to the throne of Austria-Hungary, by a Yugoslav nationalist, Gavrilo Princip in Sarajevo, June 28th 1914. This set off a diplomatic crisis when Austria-Hungary delivered an ultimatum to Serbia, and international alliances were invoked. Within weeks, the major powers were at war and the conflict soon spread around the world. By the end of the war, four major imperial powers; the German, Russian, Austro-Hungarian and Ottoman empires— ceased to exist. The map of Europe was redrawn, with several independent nations restored or created. On peace, the League of Nations formed with the aim of preventing any repetition of such an appalling conflict, encouraging cooperation and communication between the newly autonomous nation states. This laudatory pursuit failed spectacularly with the advent of the Second World War however, with new European nationalism and the rise of fascism paving the way for the next global crisis.

This book is part of the World War One Centenary series; creating, collating and reprinting new and old works of poetry, fiction, autobiography and analysis. The series forms a commemorative tribute to mark the passing of one of the world's bloodiest wars, offering new perspectives on this tragic yet fascinating period of human history.

Amelia Carruthers

A Timeline of the Major Events of World War One in Europe

1914

28th June	Franz Ferdinand Assassinated at Sarajevo.

28th June — Franz Ferdinand Assassinated at Sarajevo.

29th June — Austro-Hungary send despatch to Vienna accusing Serbian complicity in the killing.

5th July — Kaiser Wilhelm promises German support for Austria against Serbia.

20th July — Austria-Hungary sends troops to the Serbian frontier.

25th July — Serbia mobilises its troops, Russia sends troops to the Austrian frontier.

28th July — Austria-Hungary Declares war on Serbia.

29th July	Austrians bombard Belgrade and German patrols cross the French border. Britain warns it cannot remain neutral.
1st August	Germany declares war on Russia. Italy and Belgium announce neutrality. French mobilisation ordered.
3rd August	Germany declares war on France and invades Belgium (Schlieffen plan). Great Britain mobilises.
4th August	Britain declares war on Germany and Austria-Hungary (after ultimatum to stand down). US declares neutrality. Germany declares war on Belgium.
6th August	First British casualties with the HMS Amphion sunk by German mines in the North sea. 150 men dead.
7th August	First members of the BEF (British Expeditionary Force) arrive in France.

11th August	Start of enlisting for Kitchener's New Army 'Your King and Country Need You'.
20th August	Brussels is evacuated as German troops occupy the city.
23rd August	The BEF started its retreat from Mons. Germany invades France.
26th August	Russian army defeated at Tannenburg and Masurian Lakes. BEF suffers over 7000 casualties at the Battle of Le Cateau –forced to retreat.
6th September	Battle of the Marne starts; checks German advance, but at the cost of 13,000 British, 250,000 French and 250,000 German casualties.
19th October	First Battle of Ypres.
29th October	Turkey enters the war (on Germany's side).
22nd November	Trenches are now established along the entire Western Front.
8th December	Battle of the Falkland Islands.

1915

19th January	First Zeppelin raid on Britain (Great Yarmouth and Kings Lynn – killing 5).

19th January   First Zeppelin raid on Britain (Great Yarmouth and Kings Lynn – killing 5).

18th February   Blockade of Great Britain by German U-boats begins. All vessels considered viable targets, including neutrals.

22nd April   Second Battle of Ypres begins. Widespread use of poison gas by Germany.

25th April   Allied troops land in Gallipoli.

2nd May   Austro-German offensive on Galicia begins.

7th May   The Lusitania is sunk by a German U-Boat – creating US/German diplomatic crisis.

23rd May   Italy declares war on Germany and Austria

31st May   First Zeppelin raid on London, killing 35 and shaking morale.

30th June	German troops use flamethrowers for the first time, against the British at Hooge, Ypres.
5th August	Germany captures Warsaw from the Russians.
21st August	Final British offensive in the Dardanelles (Scimitar Hill, Gallipoli). They lose, and suffer 5000 deaths.
25th September	Start of the Battle of Loos and Champagne. The British use gas for the first time, but the wind blows it over their own troops, resulting in 2632 casualties.
31st October	Steel helmets introduced on the British Front.
15th December	Sir Douglas Haig replaces Sir John French as Commander of the BEF.

1916

8th January	

8th January   Allied evacuation of Helles marks the end of the Gallipoli campaign.

21st February   Start of the Battle of Verdun – German offensive against the Mort-Homme Ridge. The battle lasts 10 months and over a million men become casualties. (Finishes 18th December, the longest and costliest battle of the Western Front).

9th March   Germany declares war on Portugal. Six days later, Austria follows suit.

31st May   Battle of Jutland – lasts until 1st June. German High Seas Fleet is forced to retire despite having inflicted heavier losses on the Royal Navy (14 ships and 6,100 men). German fleet irreparably damaged.

4th June   Start of the Russian Brusilov Offensive on the Eastern front. Nearly cripples Austro-Hungary.

1st July	Start of the Battle of the Somme – 750,000 allied soldiers along a 25 mile front. Nearly 60,000 are dead or wounded on the first day.
14th July	Battle of Bazetin Ridge marks the end of the first Somme Offensive. The British break the German line but fail to deploy cavalry fast enough to take advantage. 9,000 men are lost.
23rd July	Battle of Pozières Ridge marks the second Somme Offensive, costs 17,000 allied casualties – the majority of whom are Australian. (ends 7th August).
10th August	End of the Brusilov Offensive.
9th September	The Battle of Ginchy. The British capture Ginchy – a post of vital strategic importance as it commands a view of the whole battlefield.
15th September	First use en masse of tanks at the Somme. The Battle of Flers-Courcelette signifies the start of the third stage of the Somme offensive.

13th November	Battle of Ancre. The fourth phase of the Somme Offensive is marked by the British capturing Beaumont Hamel and St. Pierre Division, taking nearly 4,000 prisoners.
12th December	Germany delivers Peace Note to Allies suggesting compromise.

1917

1st February	Germany's unrestricted submarine warfare campaign starts.
3rd February	US sever diplomatic relations with Germany as U-boats threaten US shipping. Intercepted messages reveal that Germany is provoking the Mexicans into war with the US.
21st February	The great German withdrawal begins. Serre, Miraumont, Petit Miraumont, Pys and Warlencourt are evacuated, falling back 25 miles to establish stronger positions on the Hindenburg Line.
15th March	Tsar Nicholas II abdicates as Moscow falls to Russian Revolutionaries. Demise of the Russian army frees German troops for the Western front.
6th April	USA declares war on Germany – troops mobilise immediately.

9th April	Battle of Arras. British successfully employ new tactics of creeping barrages, the 'graze fuse' and counter battery fire.
16th April	France launches an unsuccessful offensive on the Western Front. – Second Battle of Aisne begins as part of the 'Nivelle Offensive'. Losses are horrendous, triggering mutinies in the French Army.
7th June	The Battle of Messines Ridge. British succeed with few casualties, detonating 19 mines under German front lines – the explosions are reportedly heard from England.
13th June	Germans launch first major heavy bomber raid of London – kills and injures 594.
25th June	First US troops arrive in France.
31st July	Start of the Third Battle at Ypres – a 15 mile front in Flanders. Initial attacks are successful as the German forward trenches are lightly manned.

15th August	The Battle of Lens (Hill 70). – Canadians at the forefront , won a high vantage point, though loss of 9,200 men.
20th August	Third Battle of Verdun begins. French progress is marked by gaining lost territory in the earlier battles.
9th October	The third phase of the Ypres Offensive begins with British and French troops taking Poelcapelle. 25mm of rain falls in 48 hours and the battlefield turns into a quagmire.
12th October	British launch assault at Ypres Against the Passchendale Ridge. New Zealand and Australians take terrible casualties. Bogged down in mud and forced back to start lines.
24th October	Battle of Caporetto – Italian Army heavily defeated.
26th October	Second Battle of Passchendaele begins, 12,000 men lost and 300 yards gained (ends 10th November – 500,000 casualties,

140,000 deaths and 5 miles gained).

6th November   Britain launches major offensive on the Western Front.

20th November   Victory for British tanks at Cambrai - The Royal flying Corps drop bombs at the same time on German anti-tank guns and strong points. Early example of the 'Blitzkrieg' tactics later used by Germany in World War Two.

5th December   Armistice between Germany and Russia signed.

1918

16th January	Riots in Vienna and Budapest with dissatisfaction at the war.
3rd March	Treaty of Brest-Litovsk signed between (Soviet) Russia and Germany.
21st March	Second Battle of the Somme marked by the German spring offensive, the 'Kaiserschlacht'. Germans attack along a 50 mile front south of Arras.
22nd March	Victory for Germany with operation Michael - Use of new 'Storm trooper' assault to smash through British positions west of St. Quentin, taking 16,000 prisoners.
23rd March	Greatest air battle of the war takes place over the Somme, with 70 aircraft involved.
5th April	The German Spring Offensive halts outside Amiens as British and Australian forces hold the Line. The second 1917 battle of

the Somme ends, as Germany calls off operation Michael.

9th April	Germany starts offensive in Flanders –Battle of the Lys (ends 29th April).
19th May	German air force launches largest raid on London, using 33 aircraft.
27th May	Operation Blucher – The Third German Spring Offensive attacks the French army along the Aisne River. French are forced back to the Marne, but hold the river with help from the Americans.
15th July	Second battle of the Marne started; final phase of German spring offensive. Start of the collapse of the German army with irreplaceable casualties.
8th August	Second Battle of Amiens – German resistance sporadic and thousands surrender.
27th September	British offensive on the Cambrai Front leads to the storming of the Hindenburg Line. Battle of St.

Quentin – British and U.S troops launch devastating offensives.

4th October	Germany asks the allies for an armistice (sent to Woodrow Wilson).

4th October — Germany asks the allies for an armistice (sent to Woodrow Wilson).

8th October — Allies advance along a 20 mile front from St. Quentin to Cambrai, driving the Germans back and capturing 10,000 troops.

29th October — Germany's navy mutinies (at Jade).

3rd November — Austria makes peace. German sailors mutiny at Kiel.

9th November — Kaiser Wilhelm abdicates and revolution breaks out in Berlin.

11th November — Germany signs the armistice with the allies – coming into effect at 11.00am (official end of WWI).

1919

10th January	Communist Revolt in Berlin (Battle of Berlin).

10th January   Communist Revolt in Berlin
              (Battle of Berlin).

18th January   Paris Peace Conference Begins.

25th January   Principle of a League of Nations
              ratified.

6th May   Under conditions of the Peace
              conference, German colonies are
              annexed.

21st June   The surrendered German naval
              fleet at Scapa Flow was scuttled.

28th June   Treaty of Versailles signed.

19th July   Cenotaph unveiled in London.

By Amelia Carruthers

The Western Front

The First World War was one of the deadliest conflicts in history. More than seven million civilians and nine million combatants were killed, a casualty rate exacerbated by the belligerents' technological and industrial sophistication – and tactical stalemate. It lasted four years, however nobody expected the war to be more than a short, decisive battle. Following the outbreak of war in 1914, the German Army opened the Western Front by first invading Luxembourg and Belgium, then gaining military control of important industrial regions in France. Battle raged until the end of the war in 1918 when the German government sued for peace, unable to sustain the massive losses suffered. The western front included some of the bloodiest conflicts of the war, with few significant advances made; among the most costly of these offensives were the Battle of Verdun with a combined 700,000 dead, the Battle of the Somme with more than a million casualties, and the Battle of Passchendaele with roughly 600,000 casualties.

The massive tide of initial German advance was only turned with the Battle of the Marne, when the German army came within 70km of Paris. This, first battle of the Marne (5th-12th September 1914) enabled French and British troops to force the German retreat by exploiting a gap which appeared between the first and second Armies. The German army retreated north of the Aisne River and dug in there, establishing the beginnings of a static western front that was to last for the next three years.

Following this German setback, the opposing forces tried to outflank each other in the Race for the Sea, and quickly extended their trench systems from the North Sea to the Swiss frontier. As a result of this frenzied race, both sides dug in along a meandering line of fortified trenches, stretching all the way along the front - a line which remained essentially unchanged for most of the war.

Between 1915 and 1917 there were several major offensives along this front. The attacks employed massive artillery bombardments and massed infantry advances. However, a combination of entrenchments, machine gun nests, barbed wire, and artillery repeatedly inflicted severe casualties on the attackers and counterattacking defenders. In an effort to break the deadlock, the western front saw the introduction of new military technology, including poison gas, aircraft and tanks. Although all sides had signed treaties (the Hague Conventions of 1899 and 1907) which prohibited the use of chemical weapons in warfare, they were used on a large scale during the conflict. This was most evident at the Second Battle of Ypres (21 April – 25 May 1915), an offensive led by the Germans in order to disrupt Franco-British planning and test a relatively new weapon; chlorine gas. The Germans released 168 tons of this gas onto the battlefield, creating panic amongst the British soldiers - many of whom fled creating an undefended 6km wide gap in the Allied line.

The Germans were unprepared for the level of their success however and lacked sufficient reserves to exploit the opening. Canadian troops quickly arrived and drove back the German advance. It was only after the adoption of substantially revised tactics that some degree of mobility was restored to the front. The German Spring Offensive of put such ideas to good use, with recently introduced infiltration tactics, involving small, lightly equipped infantry forces attacking enemy rear areas while bypassing enemy front line strong-points and isolating them for attack by follow-up troops with heavier weapons. They advanced nearly 97km to the west, which marked the deepest advance by either side since 1914 and very nearly succeeded in forcing a breakthrough. The German Chief of Staff, Erich von Falkenhayn, believed that a breakthrough might no longer be possible, and instead focused on forcing a French capitulation by inflicting massive casualties. The new goal was to 'bleed France white.'

This policy resulted in the Battle of Verdun, which began on 21st February after a nine-day delay due to snow and blizzards. To inflict the maximum possible casualties, Falkenhayn planned to attack a position from which the French could not retreat for reason of both strategic positions and national pride - Verdun was an important stronghold, surrounded by a ring of forts, guarding the direct route to Paris. The French put up heavy resistance though, and halted the German advance by 28th February. Over the summer they slowly advanced with the use of the rolling barrages and pushed the Germans back 2km from their original position. This battle, known as the 'Mincing Machine of Verdun' became a symbol of French determination and self-sacrifice. The futility and mass slaughter of the war was perhaps nowhere better illustrated than in the Battle of the Somme however; convened to help relieve the French after their enormous losses at Verdun.

Here, British divisions in Picardy launched an attack around the river Somme, supported by five French divisions on their right flank. The attack was preceded by seven days of heavy artillery bombardment, which failed to destroy any of the German defences. This resulted in the greatest number of casualties (killed, wounded, and missing) in a single day in the history of the British army, about 57,000. By August 1916, General Haig, like Falkenhayn, concluded that a breakthrough was unlikely, and instead switched tactics to a series of small unit actions (similar to the German infiltration tactics). The final phase of the Somme also saw the first use of the tank on the battlefield, which did make early progress (4km), but they were mechanically unreliable and ultimately failed. All told, the battle which lasted five months only succeeded in advancing eight kilometres, at a truly massive loss to life. The British had suffered about 420,000 casualties and the French around 200,000. It is estimated that the Germans lost 465,000, although this figure is controversial.

This constant loss of life meant that troop morale became incredibly low. The Nivelle Offensive, primarily including French and Russian troops - which promised to end the war within forty-eight hours, was significant failure. It took place on rough, upward sloping terrain, tiring the men - whose troubles were increased due to poor intelligence and German control of the skies. Within a week, 100,000 French troops were dead and on 3rd May, an entire division refused their orders to march, arriving drunk and without their weapons. Mutinies then spread and afflicted a further fifty-four French divisions, only stopped by mass arrests and trials. Such low morale was further dampened by the German's final spring offensives which very nearly succeeded in driving the allies apart

Operation Michael (March 1918), the first of these German offensives advanced 100 km, getting within shelling distance of Paris for the first time since 1914. The allies responded with vigour however, with a counter-offensive at the Marne, followed by an attack at Amiens to the North. This attack included Franco-British forces, and was spearheaded by Australian and Canadian troops, along with 600 tanks and supported by 800 aircraft. The assault proved highly successful, leading Hindenburg to name 8 August as the 'Black Day of the German Army.' These losses persuaded the German government to sue for armistice, and the Hundred Days Offensive (beginning in August 1918) proved the final straw. Many German troops surrendered, although fighting did continue until the armistice was signed on 11th November 1918. The war in the Western Front's trenches left a generation of maimed soldiers and grieved populations, though proved a decisive theatre in ending the First World War. The repercussions of this bloody conflict are still being felt to this day. It is hoped the current reader is encouraged to find out more, and enjoys this book.

Amelia Carruthers

In Flanders Fields

In Flanders fields the poppies blow
Between the crosses, row on row,
That mark our place; and in the sky
The larks, still bravely singing, fly
Scarce heard amid the guns below.

We are the Dead. Short days ago
We lived, felt dawn, saw sunset glow,
Loved and were loved, and now we lie
In Flanders fields.

Take up our quarrel with the foe:
To you from failing hands we throw
The torch; be yours to hold it high.
If ye break faith with us who die
We shall not sleep, though poppies grow
In Flanders fields.

John McCrae, May 1915

Image 1. Belgian artillery battery in action

"The War was decided in the first twenty days of fighting, and all that happened afterwards consisted in battles which, however formidable and devastating, were but desperate and vain appeals against the decision of Fate."

Winston Churchill (1874–1965), British statesman, writer. Liaison 1914, preface, E.L. Spears (1930).

.

Fighting in Flanders

To My Friends The Belgians

"I have eaten your bread and salt;
I have drunk your water and wine;
The deaths you died I have sat beside
And the lives that you led were mine."

RUDYARD KIPLING.

Foreword

Nothing is more unwise, on general principles, than to attempt to write about a war before that war is finished and before history has given it the justice of perspective. The campaign which began with the flight of the Belgian Government from Brussels and which culminated in the fall of Antwerp formed, however, a separate and distinct phase of the Greatest of Wars, and I feel that I should write of that campaign while its events are still sharp and clear in my memory and before the impressions it produced have begun to fade. I hope that those in search of a detailed or technical account of the campaign in Flanders will not read this book, because they are certain to be disappointed. It contains nothing about strategy or tactics and few military lessons can be drawn from it. It is merely the story, in simple words, of what I, a professional onlooker, who was accorded rather exceptional facilities for observation, saw in Belgium during that nation's hour of trial.

An American, I went to Belgium at the beginning of the war with an open mind. I had few, if any, prejudices. I knew the English, the French, the Belgians, the Germans equally well. I had friends in all four countries and many happy recollections of days I had spent in each. When I left Antwerp after the German occupation

I was as pro-Belgian as though I had been born under the red-black-and- yellow banner. I had seen a country, one of the loveliest and most peaceable in Europe, invaded by a ruthless and brutal soldiery; I had seen its towns and cities blackened by fire and broken by shell; I had seen its churches and its historic monuments destroyed; I had seen its highways crowded with hunted, homeless fugitives; I had seen its fertile fields strewn with the corpses of what had once been the manhood of the nation; I had seen its women left husbandless and its children left fatherless; I had seen what was once a Garden of the Lord turned into a land of desolation; and I had seen its people--a people whom I, like the rest of the world, had always thought of as pleasure-loving, inefficient, easy-going--I had seen this people, I say, aroused, resourceful, unafraid, and fighting, fighting, fighting. Do you wonder that they captured my imagination, that they won my admiration? I am pro-Belgian; I admit it frankly. I should be ashamed to be anything else.

E. Alexander Powell
London, November 1, 1914.

Mr. Powell (at right) and his photographer, Donald Thompson. Thompson was a little, wiry man who looked, sartorially as well as physically, as though he had been born on horseback

I. The War Correspondents

War correspondents regard war very much as a doctor regards sickness. I don't suppose that a doctor is actually glad that people are sick, but so long as sickness exists in the world he feels that he might as well get the benefit of it. It is the same with war correspondents. They do not wish anyone to be killed on their account, but so long as men are going to be killed anyway, they want to be on hand to witness the killing and, through the newspapers, to tell the world about it. The moment that the war broke out, therefore, a veritable army of British and American correspondents descended upon the Continent. Some of them were men of experience and discretion who had seen many wars and had a right to wear on their jackets more campaign ribbons than most generals. These men took the war seriously. They were there to get the news and, at no matter what expenditure of effort and money, to get that news to the end of a telegraph-wire so that the people in England and America might read it over their coffee-cups the next morning. These men had unlimited funds at their disposal; they had the united influence of thousands of newspapers and of millions of newspaper-readers solidly behind them; and they carried in their pockets letters of introduction from editors and ex-presidents and ambassadors and prime ministers.

Then there was an army corps of special writers, many of them with well-known names, sent out by various newspapers and magazines to write "mail stuff," as dispatches which are sent by mail instead of telegraph are termed, and "human interest" stories. Their qualifications for reporting the greatest war in history consisted, for the most part, in having successfully "covered" labour troubles and murder trials and coronations and presidential conventions, and, in a few cases, Central American revolutions. Most of the stories which they sent home were written in comfortable hotel rooms in London or Paris or Rotterdam or Ostend. One of these correspondents, however, was not content with a hotel window viewpoint. He wanted to see some German soldiers--preferably Uhlans. So he obtained a letter of introduction to some people living in the neighbourhood of Courtrai, on the Franco-Belgian frontier. He made his way there with considerable difficulty and received a cordial welcome. The very first night that he was there a squadron of Uhlans galloped into the town, there was a slight skirmish, and they galloped out again. The correspondent, who was a sound sleeper, did not wake up until it was all over. Then he learned that the Uhlans had ridden under his very window.

Crossing on the same steamer with me from New York was a well- known novelist who in his spare time edits a Chicago newspaper. He was provided with a sheaf of introductions from exalted personages and a bag containing a thousand pounds in gold coin. It was so heavy that he had brought a man along to help him carry it, and at night they took turns in sitting up and guarding it. He confided to me that he had spent most of his life in trying to see wars, but though on four occasions he had travelled many thousands of miles to countries where wars were in progress, each time he had arrived just after the last shot was fired. He assured me very earnestly that he would go back to Michigan Boulevard quite contentedly if he could see just one battle. I am glad to say that his perseverance was finally rewarded and that he saw his battle. He never told me just how much of the thousand pounds he took back to Chicago with him, but from some remarks he let drop I gathered that he had found battle-hunting an expensive pastime.

One of the great London dailies was represented in Belgium by a young and slender and very beautiful English girl whose name, as a novelist and playwright, is known on both sides of the Atlantic. I met her in the American Consulate at Ghent, where she was pleading with Vice-Consul Van Hee to assist her in getting through the German lines to Brussels. She had heard a rumour that Brussels was shortly going to be burned or sacked or something of the sort, and she wanted to be on hand for the burning and sacking. She had arrived in Belgium wearing a London tailor's idea of what constituted a suitable costume for a war correspondent-- perhaps I should say war correspondentess. Her luggage was a model of compactness: it consisted of a sleeping-bag, a notebook, half a dozen pencils--and a powder-puff. She explained that she brought the sleeping-bag because she understood that war correspondents always slept in the field. As most of the fields in that part of Flanders were just then under several inches of water as a result of the autumn rains, a folding canoe would have been more useful. She was as insistent on being taken to see a battle as a child is on being taken to the pantomime. Eventually her pleadings got the better of my judgment and I took her out in the car towards Alost to see, from a safe distance, what promised to be a small cavalry engagement. But the Belgian cavalry unexpectedly ran into a heavy force of Germans, and before we realized what was happening we were in a very warm corner indeed. Bullets were kicking up little spurts of dust about us; bullets were tang-tanging through the trees and clipping off twigs, which fell down upon our heads; the rat-tat-tat of the German musketry was answered by the angry snarl of the Belgian machine-guns; in a field near by the bodies of two recently killed cuirassiers lay sprawled grotesquely. The Belgian troopers were stretched flat upon the ground, a veteran English correspondent was giving a remarkable imitation of the bark on a tree, and my driver, my photographer and I were peering cautiously from behind the corner of a brick farmhouse. I supposed that Miss War Correspondent was there too, but when I turned to speak to her she was gone. She was standing beside the car, which we had left in the middle of the road because the bullets were flying too thickly to turn it around, dabbing at her nose with a powder-puff which she had left in the tonneau and then critically examining the effect in a pocket-mirror.

"For the love of God!" said I, running out and dragging her back to shelter, "don't you know that you'll be killed if you stay out here?"

"Will I?" said she, sweetly. "Well, you surely don't expect me to be killed with my nose unpowdered, do you?"

That evening I asked her for her impressions of her first battle.

"Well," she answered, after a meditative pause, "it certainly was very chic."

The third and largest division of this journalistic army consisted of free lances who went to the Continent at their own expense on the chance of "stumbling into something." About the only thing that any of them stumbled into was trouble. Some of them bore the most extraordinary credentials ever carried by a correspondent; some of them had no credentials at all. One gentleman, who was halted while endeavouring to reach the firing line in a decrepit cab, informed the officer before whom he was taken that he represented the Ladies' Home Journal of Philadelphia. Another displayed a letter from the editor of a well-known magazine saying that he "would be pleased to consider any articles which you care to submit." A third, upon being questioned, said naively that he represented his literary agent. Then--I almost forgot him--there was a Methodist clergyman from Boston who explained to the Provost-Marshal that he was gathering material for a series of sermons on the horrors of war. Add to this army of writers another army of photographers and war- artists and cinematograph-operators and you will have some idea of the problem with which the military authorities of the warring nations were confronted. It finally got down to the question of which should be permitted to remain in the field--the war correspondents or the soldiers. There wasn't room for them both. It was decided to retain the soldiers.

The general staffs of the various armies handled the war correspondent problem in different ways. The British War Office at first announced that under no considerations would any correspondents be permitted in the areas where British troops were operating, but such a howl went up from Press and public alike that this order was modified and it was announced that a limited number of correspondents, representing the great newspaper syndicates and press associations, would, after fulfilling certain rigorous requirements, be permitted to accompany his Majesty's forces in the field. These fortunate few having been chosen after much heart-burning, they proceeded to provide themselves with the prescribed uniforms and field-kits, and some of them even purchased horses. After the war had been in progress for three months they were still in London. The French General Staff likewise announced that no correspondents would be permitted with the armies, and when any were caught they were unceremoniously shipped to the nearest port between two unsympathetic gendarmes with a warning that they would be shot if they were caught again.

The Belgian General Staff made no announcement at all. The police merely told those correspondents who succeeded in getting into the fortified position of Antwerp that their room was preferable to their company and informed them at what hour the next train for the Dutch frontier was leaving. Now the correspondents knew perfectly well that neither the British nor the French nor the Belgians would actually shoot them, if for no other reason than the unfavourable impression which would be produced by such a proceeding; but they did know that if they tried the patience of the military authorities too far they would spend the rest of the war in a military prison. So, as an imprisoned correspondent is as valueless to the newspaper which employs him as a prisoner of war is to the nation whose uniform he wears, they compromised by picking up such information as they could along the edge of things. Which accounts for most of the dispatches being dated from Ostend or Ghent or Dunkirk or Boulogne or from "the back of the front," as one correspondent ingeniously put it.

As for the Germans, they said bluntly that any correspondents found within their lines would be treated as spies--which meant being blindfolded and placed between a stone wall and a firing party. And every correspondent knew that they would do exactly what they said. They have no proper respect for the Press, these Germans.

That I was officially recognized by the Belgian Government and given a laisser-passer by the military

Governor of Antwerp permitting me to pass at will through both the outer and inner lines of fortifications, that a motor-car and a military driver were placed at my disposal, and that throughout the campaign in Flanders I was permitted to accompany the Belgian forces, was not due to any peculiar merits or qualifications of my own, or even to the influence exerted by the powerful paper which I represented, but to a series of unusual and fortunate circumstances which there is no need to detail here. There were many correspondents who merited from sheer hard work what I received as a result of extraordinary good fortune.

The civilians who were wandering, foot-loose and free, about the theatre of operations were by no means confined to the representatives of the Press; there was an amazing number of young Englishmen and Americans who described themselves as "attaches" and "consular couriers" and "diplomatic messengers," and who intimated that they were engaged in all sorts of dangerous and important missions. Many of these were adventurous young men of means who had "come over to see the fun" and who had induced the American diplomatic representatives in London and The Hague to give them dispatches of more or less importance-- usually less than more--to carry through to Antwerp and Brussels. In at least one instance the official envelopes with the big red seals which they so ostentatiously displayed contained nothing but sheets of blank paper. Their sole motive was in nearly all cases curiosity. They had no more business wandering about the war-zone than they would have had wandering about a hospital where men were dying. Belgium was being slowly strangled; her villages had been burned, her fields laid waste, her capital was in the hands of the enemy, her people were battling for their national existence; yet these young men came in and demanded first-row seats, precisely as though the war was a spectacle which was being staged for their special benefit.

One youth, who in his busy moments practised law in Boston, though quite frankly admitting that he was only actuated by curiosity, was exceedingly angry with me because I declined to take him to the firing-line. He seemed to regard the desperate battle which was then in progress for the possession of Antwerp very much as though it was a football game in the Harvard stadium; he seemed to think that he had a right to see it. He said that he had come all the way from Boston to see a battle, and when I remained firm in my refusal to take him to the front he intimated quite plainly that I was no gentleman and that nothing would give him greater pleasure than to have a shell explode in my immediate vicinity.

For all its grimness, the war was productive of more than one amusing episode. I remember a mysterious stranger who called one morning on the American Consul at Ostend to ask for assistance in getting through to Brussels. When the Consul asked him to be seated he bowed stiffly and declined, and when a seat was again urged upon him he explained, in a hoarse whisper, that sewn in his trousers were two thousand pounds in bank-notes which he was taking through to Brussels for the relief of stranded English and Americans--hence he couldn't very well sit down.

Of all the horde of adventurous characters who were drawn to the Continent on the outbreak of war as iron-filings are attracted by a magnet, I doubt if there was a more picturesque figure than a little photographer from Kansas named Donald Thompson. I met him first while paying a flying visit to Ostend. He blew into the Consulate there wearing an American army shirt, a pair of British officer's riding-breeches, French puttees and a Highlander's forage-cap, and carrying a camera the size of a parlour-phonograph. No one but an American could have accomplished what he had, and no American but one from Kansas. He had not only seen war, all military prohibitions to the contrary, but he had actually photographed it.

Thompson is a little man, built like Harry Lauder; hard as nails, tough as raw hide, his skin tanned to the colour of a well-smoked meerschaum, and his face perpetually wreathed in what he called his "sunflower smile." He affects riding-breeches and leather leggings and looks, physically as well as sartorially, as though he had been born on horseback. He has more chilled steel nerve than any man I know, and before he had been in Belgium a month his name became a synonym throughout the army for coolness and daring. He reached Europe on a tramp-steamer with an overcoat, a toothbrush, two clean handkerchiefs, and three large cameras. He expected to have some of them confiscated or broken, he explained, so he brought along three as a measure of precaution. His cameras were the largest size made. "By using a big camera no one can possibly accuse me of being a spy," he explained ingenuously. His papers consisted of an American passport, a certificate of membership in the Benevolent and Protective Order of Elks, and a letter from Colonel Sam Hughes, Canadian Minister of Militia, authorizing him to take pictures of Canadian troops wherever found.

Thompson made nine attempts to get from Paris to the front. He was arrested eight times and spent eight nights in guard-houses. Each time he was taken before a military tribunal. Utterly ignoring the subordinates, he would insist on seeing the officer in command. He would grasp the astonished Frenchman by the hand and inquire solicitously after his health and that of his family.

"How many languages do you speak?" I asked him.

"Three," said he. "English, American, and Yankee."

On one occasion he commandeered a motorcycle standing outside a cafe and rode it until the petrol ran out, whereupon he abandoned it by the roadside and pushed on afoot. On another occasion he explained to the French officer who arrested him that he was endeavouring to rescue his wife and children, who were in the hands of the Germans somewhere on the Belgian frontier. The officer was so affected by the pathos of the story that he gave Thompson a lift in his car. As a matter of fact, Thompson's wife and family were quite safe in Topeka, Kansas. Whenever he was stopped by patrols he would display his letter from the Minister of Militia and explain that he was trying to overtake the Canadian troops. "Vive le Canada!" the French would shout enthusiastically. "Hurrah for our brave allies, les Canadiens! They are doubtless with the British at the front"--and permit him to proceed. Thompson did not think it necessary to inform them that the nearest Canadian troops were still at Quebec.

When within sound of the German guns he was arrested for the eighth time and sent to Amiens escorted by two gendarmes, who were ordered to see him aboard the first train for Boulogne. They evidently considered that they had followed instructions when they saw him buy a through ticket for London. Shortly after midnight a train loaded with wounded pulled into the station. Assisted by some British soldiers, Thompson scrambled to the top of a train standing at the next platform and made a flashlight picture. A wild panic ensued in the crowded station. It was thought that a German bomb had exploded. Thompson was pulled down by the police and would have been roughly handled had it not been for the interference of his British friends, who said that he belonged to their regiment. Shortly afterwards a train loaded with artillery which was being rushed to the front came in. Thompson, once more aided and abetted by the British Tommies, slipped under the tarpaulin covering a field-gun and promptly fell asleep. When he awoke the next morning he was at Mons. A regiment of Highlanders was passing. He exchanged a cake of chocolate for a fatigue-cap and fell in with them. After marching for two hours the regiment was ordered into the trenches. Thompson went into the trenches too. All through that terrible day Thompson plied his trade as the soldiers plied theirs. They used their rifles and he used his camera. Men were shot dead on either side of him. A storm of shrapnel shrieked and howled overhead. He said that the fire of the German artillery was amazingly accurate and rapid. They would concentrate their entire fire on a single regiment or battery and when that regiment or battery was out of action they would turn to another and do the same thing over again. When the British fell back before the German onset Thompson remained in the trenches long enough to get pictures of the charging Germans. Then he ran for his life.

That night he bivouacked with a French line regiment, the men giving him food and a blanket. The next morning he set out for Amiens en route for England. As the train for Boulogne, packed to the doors with refugees, was pulling out of the Amiens station, he noticed a first-class compartment marked "Reserved," the only occupant being a smartly gowned young woman. Thompson said that she was very good-looking. The train was moving, but Thompson took a running jump and dived head-foremost through the window, landing in the lady's lap. She was considerably startled until he said that he was an American. That seemed to explain everything. The young woman proved to be a Russian countesss who had been living in Paris and who was returning, via England, to Petrograd. The French Government had placed a compartment at her disposal, but in the jam at the Paris station she had become separated from her maid, who had the bag containing her money. Thompson recounted his adventures at Mons and asked her if she would smuggle his films into England concealed on her person, as he knew from previous experience that he would be stopped and searched by Scotland Yard detectives when the train reached Boulogne and that, in all probability, the films would be confiscated or else held up so long that they would be valueless. The countess finally consented, but suggested, in return for the danger she was incurring, that Thompson lend her a thousand francs, which she would return as soon as she reached London. As he had with him only two hundred and fifty francs, he paid her the balance in United Cigar Stores coupons, some of which he chanced to have in his pocket-book, and which, he explained, was American war currency. He told me that he gave her almost enough to get a briar-pipe. At Boulogne he was arrested, as he had foreseen, was stripped, searched and his camera opened, but as nothing was found he was permitted to continue to London, where he went to the countess's hotel and received his films--and, I might add, his money and cigar coupons. Two hours later, having posted his films to America, he was on his way to Belgium.

Landing at Ostend, he managed to get by train as far as Malines. He then started to walk the twenty-odd miles into Brussels, carrying his huge camera, his overcoat, field-glasses, and three hundred films. When ten miles down the highway a patrol of Uhlans suddenly spurred out from behind a hedge and covered him with their pistols. Thompson promptly pulled a little silk American flag out of his pocket and shouted "Hoch der Kaiser!" and "Auf wiedersehn" which constituted his entire stock of German. Upon being examined by the officer in command of the German outpost, he explained that his Canadian credentials were merely a blind to get through the lines of the Allies and that he really represented a syndicate of German newspapers in America, whereupon he was released with apologies and given a seat in an ambulance which was going into Brussels. As his funds were by this time running low, he started out to look for inexpensive lodgings. As he remarked to me, "I thought we had some pretty big house-agents out in Kansas, but this Mr. 'A. Louer' has them beaten a mile. Why, that fellow has his card on every house that's for rent in Brussels!"

The next morning, while chatting with a pretty English girl in front of a cafe, a German officer who was passing ordered his arrest as a spy. "All right," said Thompson, "I'm used to being arrested, but would you mind waiting just a minute until I get your picture?" The German, who had no sense of humour, promptly smashed the camera with his sword. Despite Thompson's protestations that he was an inoffensive American, the Germans destroyed all his films and ordered him to be out of the city before six that evening. He walked the thirty miles to Ghent and there caught a train for Ostend to get one of his reserve cameras, which he had cached there. When I met him in Ostend he said that he had been there overnight, that he was tired of a quiet life and was looking for action, so I took him back with me to Antwerp. The Belgians had made an inflexible rule that no photographers would be permitted with the army, but before Thompson had been in Antwerp twenty-four hours he had obtained permission from the Chief of the General Staff himself to take pictures when and where he pleased. Thompson remained with me until the fall of Antwerp and the German occupation, and no man could have had a more loyal or devoted companion. It is no exaggeration to say that he saw more of the campaign in Flanders than any individual, military or civilian--"le Capitaine Thompson," as he came to be known, being a familiar and popular figure on the Belgian battle-line.

Strauss, the Belgo-American who was decorated by the King for bravery in the armoured-car raid in which the Prince de Ligne was killed

There is one other person of whom passing mention should be made, if for no other reason than because his name will appear from time to time in this narrative. I take pleasure, therefore, in introducing you to M. Marcel Roos, the young Belgian gentleman who drove my motor-car. When war was declared, Roos, who belonged to the jeunesse doree of Brussels, gave his own ninety horse-power car to the Government and enlisted in a regiment of grenadiers. Because he was as familiar with

the highways and byways of Belgium as a housewife is
with her kitchen, and because he spoke English, French,
Flemish and German, he was detailed to drive the car
which the Belgian Government placed at my disposal.
He was as big and loyal and good-natured as a St.
Bernard dog and he was as cool in danger as Thompson--
which is the highest compliment I can pay him.
Incidentally, he was the most successful forager that I
have ever seen; more than once, in villages which had
apparently been swept clean of everything edible by the
Belgians or the Germans, he produced quite an excellent
dinner as mysteriously as a conjuror produces rabbits
from a hat.

Now you must bear in mind that although one
could get into Antwerp with comparative ease, it by no
means followed that one could get out to the firing-line.
A long procession of correspondents came to Antwerp
and remained a day or so and then went away again
without once getting beyond the city gates. Even if one
succeeded in obtaining the necessary laisser-passer from
the military Government, there was no way of reaching
the front, as all the automobiles and all except the most
decrepit horses had been requisitioned for the use of the
army. There was, you understand, no such thing as
hiring an automobile, or even buying one. Even the few
people who had influence enough to retain their cars

found them useless, as one of the very first acts of the military authorities was to commandeer the entire supply of petrol. The bulk of the cars were used in the ambulance service or for purposes of transport, the army train consisting entirely of motor vehicles. Staff officers, certain Government officials, and members of the diplomatic and consular corps were provided by the Government with automobiles and military drivers. Every one else walked or used the trams. Thus it frequently happened that a young staff officer, who had never before known the joys of motoring, would tear madly down the street in a luxurious limousine, his spurred boots resting on the broadcloth cushions, while the ci-devant owner of the car, who might be a banker or a merchant prince, would jump for the side-walk to escape being run down. With the declaration of war and the taking over of all automobiles by the military, all speed laws were flung to the winds.

No matter how unimportant his business, every one tore through the city streets as though the devil (or the Germans) were behind him. The staid citizens of Antwerp quickly developed a remarkably agility in getting out of the way of furiously driven cars. They had to. Otherwise they would have been killed.

Because, from the middle of August to the middle of October, Antwerp was the capital of Belgium and the seat of the King, Cabinet, and diplomatic corps; because from it any point on the battle-front could easily be reached by motor-car; and because, above all else, it was at the end of the cable and the one place in Belgium where there was any certainty of dispatches getting through to England, I made it my headquarters during the operations in Flanders, going out to the front in the morning and returning to the Hotel St. Antoine at night. I doubt if war correspondence has ever been carried on under such comfortable, even luxurious, conditions. "Going out to the front" became as commonplace a proceeding as for a business man to take the morning train to the city. For one whose previous campaigning had been done in Persia, Mexico and North Africa and the Balkans, it was a novel experience to leave a large and fashionable hotel after breakfast, take a run of twenty or thirty miles over stone-paved roads in a powerful and comfortable car, witness a battle--provided, of course, that there happened to be a battle on that day's list of events--and get back to the hotel in time to dress for dinner. Imagine it, if you please! Imagine leaving a line of battle, where shells were shrieking overhead and musketry was crackling along the trenches, and moaning, blood-smeared figures were being placed in ambulances, and other blood-smeared figures who no longer moaned were sprawled in strange attitudes upon the ground -- imagine leaving such a scene, I say, and in an hour, or even less, finding oneself in a hotel where men and women in evening dress were dining by the light of pink-shaded candles, or in the marble- paved palm court were sipping coffee and liqueurs to the sound of water splashing gently in a fountain.

The King of the Belgians

II. The City of Gloom

In order to grasp the true significance of the events which preceded and led up to the fall of Antwerp, it is necessary to understand the extraordinary conditions which existed in and around that city when I reached there in the middle of August. At that time all that was left to the Belgians of Belgium were the provinces of Limbourg, Antwerp, and East and West Flanders. Everything else was in the possession of the Germans. Suppose, for the sake of, having things quite clear, that you unfold the map of Belgium. Now, with your pencil, draw a line across the country from east to west, starting at the Dutch city of Maastricht and passing through Hasselt, Diest, Aerschot, Malines, Alost, and Courtrai to the French frontier. This line was, roughly speaking, "the front," and for upwards of two months fighting of a more or less serious character took place along its entire length. During August and the early part of September this fighting consisted, for the most part, of attempts by the Belgian field army to harass the enemy and to threaten his lines of communication and of counter-attacks by the Germans, during which Aerschot, Malines, Sempst, and Termonde repeatedly changed hands. Some twenty miles or so behind this line was the great fortified position of Antwerp, its outer chain of

Fighting in Flanders

forts enclosing an area with a radius of nearly fifteen miles.

Antwerp, with its population of four hundred thousand souls, its labyrinth of dim and winding streets lined by mediaeval houses, and its splendid modern boulevards, lies on the east bank of the Scheldt, about fifteen miles from Dutch territorial waters, at a hairpin-turn in the river. The defences of the city were modern, extensive, and generally believed, even by military experts, to be little short of impregnable. In fact, Antwerp was almost universally considered one of the three or four strongest fortified positions in Europe. In order to capture the city it would be necessary for an enemy to break through four distinct lines of defence, any one of which, it was believed, was strong enough to oppose successfully any force which could be brought against it. The outermost line of forts began at Lierre, a dozen miles to the south-east of the city, and swept in a great quarter-circle, through Wavre-St. Catherine, Waelhem, Heyndonck and Willebroeck, to the Scheldt at Ruppelmonde.

Two or three miles behind this outer line of forts a second line of defence was formed by the Ruppel and the Nethe, which, together with the Scheldt, make a great natural waterway around three sides of the city. Back of

59

these rivers, again, was a second chain of forts completely encircling the city on a five-mile radius. The moment that the first German soldier set his foot on Belgian soil the military authorities began the herculean task of clearing of trees and buildings a great zone lying between this inner circle of forts and the city ramparts in order that an investing force might have no cover. It is estimated that within a fortnight the Belgian sappers and engineers destroyed property to the value of £16,000,000. Not San Francisco after the earthquake, nor Dayton after the flood, nor Salem after the fire presented scenes of more complete desolation than did the suburbs of Antwerp after the soldiers had finished with them.

On August 1, 1914, no city in all Europe could boast of more beautiful suburbs than Antwerp. Hidden amid the foliage of great wooded parks were stately chateaux; splendid country-houses rose from amid acres of green plush lawns and blazing gardens; the network of roads and avenues and bridle-paths were lined with venerable trees, whose branches, meeting overhead, formed leafy tunnels; scattered here and there were quaint old-world villages, with plaster walls and pottery roofs and lichen-covered church spires. By the last day of August all this had disappeared. The loveliest suburbs in Europe had been wiped from the earth as a sponge wipes figures from a slate. Every house and church and windmill, every tree and hedge and wall, in a zone some two or three miles wide by twenty long, was literally levelled to the ground. For mile after mile the splendid trees which lined the highroads were ruthlessly cut down; mansions which could fittingly have housed a king were dynamited; churches whose walls had echoed to the tramp of the Duke of Alba's mail-clad men-at-arms were levelled; villages whose picturesqueness was the joy of artists and travellers were given over to the flames. Certainly not since the burning of Moscow has there been witnessed such a scene of self-inflicted desolation. When the work of the engineers was finished a jack-rabbit could not have approached the forts without being seen. When the work of levelling had been completed, acres upon acres of barbed-wire entanglements were constructed, the wires being grounded and connected with the city lighting system so that a voltage could instantly be turned on which would prove as deadly as the electric chair at Sing Sing. Thousands of men were set to work sharpening stakes and driving these stakes, point upward, in the ground, so as to impale any soldiers who fell upon them. In front of the stakes were "man-traps," thousands of barrels with their heads knocked out being set in the ground and then covered with a thin layer of laths and earth, which would suddenly give way if a man walked upon it and drop him into the hole below. And beyond the zones of entanglements and chevaux de frise and man-traps the beet and potato-fields were sown with mines which were to be exploded by electricity when the enemy was fairly over them, and blow that enemy, whole regiments at a time, into eternity. Stretching across the fields and meadows were what looked at first glance like enormous red-brown serpents but which proved, upon closer inspection, to be trenches for infantry. The region to the south of Antwerp is a network of canals, and on the bank of every canal rose, as though by magic, parapets of sandbags. Charges of dynamite were placed under every bridge and viaduct and tunnel. Barricades of paving-stones and mattresses and sometimes farm carts were built across the highways. At certain points wires were stretched across the roads at the height of a man's head for the purpose of preventing sudden dashes by armoured motor-cars. The walls of such buildings as were left standing were loopholed for musketry. Machine-guns and quick-firers were mounted everywhere. At night the white beams of the searchlights swept this zone of desolation and turned it into day. Now the pitiable thing about it was that all this enormous destruction proved to have been wrought for nothing, for the Germans, instead of throwing huge masses of infantry against the forts, as it was anticipated that they would do, and thus giving the entanglements and the mine-fields and the machine-guns a chance to get in their work, methodically pounded the forts to pieces with siege-guns stationed a dozen miles away. In fact, when the Germans entered Antwerp not a strand of barbed wire had been cut, not a barricade defended, not a mine exploded. This, mind you, was not due to any lack of bravery on the part of the Belgians--Heaven knows, they did not lack for that !--but to the fact that the Germans never gave them a chance to make use of these elaborate and ingenious devices. It was like a man letting a child painstakingly construct an edifice of building-blocks and then, when it was completed, suddenly sweeping it aside with his hand.

As a result of these elaborate precautions, it was as difficult to go in or out of Antwerp as it is popularly supposed to be for a millionaire to enter the kingdom of Heaven. Sentries were as thick as policemen in Piccadilly. You could not proceed a quarter of a mile along any road, in any direction, without being halted by a harsh "Qui vive?" and having the business end of a rifle turned in your direction. If your papers were not in order you were promptly turned back--or arrested as a suspicious character and taken before an officer for examination-- though if you were sufficiently in the confidence of the military authorities to be given the password, you were usually permitted to pass without further question. It was some time before I lost the thrill of novelty and excitement produced by this halt-who- goes-there-advance-friend-and-give-the-countersign business. It was so exactly the sort of thing that, as a boy, I used to read about in books by George A. Henty that it seemed improbable and unreal. When we were motoring at night and a peremptory challenge would come from out the darkness and the lamps of the car would pick out the cloaked figure of the sentry as the spotlight picks out the figure of an actor on the stage, and I would lean forward and whisper the magic mot d'ordre, I always had the feeling that I was taking part in a play-which was not so very far from the truth, for, though I did not appreciate it at the time, we were all actors, more or less important, in the greatest drama ever staged.

Officers of the Guides, the crack cavalry organization of Belgium. With their fur busbies, their green jackets, and their cherry-coloured breeches, they looked like the soldiers of Napoleon

In the immediate vicinity of Antwerp the sentries were soldiers of the regular army and understood a sentry's duties, but in the outlying districts, particularly between Ostend and Ghent, the roads were patrolled by members of the Garde civique, all of whom seemed imbued with the idea that the safety of the nation depended upon their vigilance, which was a very commendable and proper attitude indeed. When I was challenged by a Garde civique I was always a little nervous, and wasted no time whatever in jamming on the brakes, because the poor fellows were nearly always excited and handled their rifles in a fashion which was far from being reassuring. More than once, while travelling in the outlying districts, we were challenged by civil guards who evidently had not been entrusted with the password, but who, when it was whispered to them, would nod their heads importantly and tell us to pass on.

"The next sentry that we meet," I said to Roos on one of these occasions, "probably has no idea of the password. I'll bet you a box of cigars that I can give him any word that comes into my head and that he won't know the difference."

As we rolled over the ancient drawbridge which gives admittance to sleepy Bruges, a bespectacled sentry, who looked as though he had suddenly been called from an accountant's desk to perform the duties of a soldier, held up his hand, palm outward, which is the signal to stop the world over.

"Halt!" he commanded quaveringly. "Advance slowly and give the word."

I leaned out as the car came opposite him. "Kalamazoo," I whispered. The next instant I was looking into the muzzle of his rifle.

"Hands up!" he shouted, and there was no longer any quaver in his voice. "That is not the word. I shouldn't be surprised if you were German spies. Get out of the car!"

It took half an hour of explanations to convince him that we were not German spies, that we really did know the password, and that we were merely having a joke-- though not, as we had planned, at his expense.

Belgian dog batteries. The machine-gun batteries drawn by dog teams rendered splendid service throughout the campaign in Flanders

The force of citizen soldiery known as the Garde civique has, so far as I am aware, no exact counterpart in any other country. It is composed of business and professional men whose chief duties, prior to the war, had been to show themselves on occasions of ceremony arrayed in gorgeous uniforms, which varied according to the province. The mounted division of the Antwerp Garde civique wore a green and scarlet uniform which resembled as closely as possible that of the Guides, the crack cavalry corps of the Belgian army. In the Flemish towns the civil guards wore a blue coat, so long in the skirts that it had to be buttoned back to permit of their walking, and a hat of stiff black felt, resembling a bowler, with a feather stuck rakishly in the band. Early in the war the Germans announced that they would not recognize the Gardes civique as combatants, and that any of them who were captured while fighting would meet with the same fate as armed civilians. This drastic ruling resulted in many amusing episodes. When it was learned that the Germans were approaching Ghent, sixteen hundred civil guardsmen threw their rifles into the canal and, stripping off their uniforms, ran about in the pink and light-blue under-garments which the Belgians affect, frantically begging the townspeople to lend them civilian clothing. As a whole, however, these citizen-soldiers did admirable service, guarding the roads, tunnels and bridges, assisting the refugees, preserving order in the towns, and, in Antwerp, taking entire charge of provisioning the army.

A fourteen-year-old boy scout who, as an officer's orderly, was present at every battle from the occupation of Brussels to the fall of Antwerp

No account of Antwerp in war time would be complete without at least passing mention of the boy scouts, who were one of the city's most picturesque and interesting features. I don't quite know how the city could have got along without them. They were always on the job; they were to be seen everywhere and they did everything. They acted as messengers, as doorkeepers, as guides, as orderlies for staff officers, and as couriers for the various ministries; they ran the elevators in the hotels, they worked in the hospitals, they assisted the refugees to find food and lodgings. The boy scouts stationed at the various ministries were on duty twenty-four hours at a stretch. They slept rolled up in blankets on the floors; they obtained their meals where and when they could and paid for them themselves, and made themselves extremely useful. If you possessed sufficient influence to obtain a motor-car, a boy scout was generally detailed to sit beside the driver and open the door and act as a sort of orderly. I had one. His name was Joseph. He was most picturesque. He wore a sombrero with a cherry-coloured puggaree and a bottle-green cape, and his green stockings turned over at the top so as to show knees as white and shapely as those of a woman. To tell the truth, however, I had nothing for him to do. So when I was not out in the car he occupied himself in running the lift at the Hotel St. Antoine. Joseph was with me during the German attack on Waelhem. We were caught in a much hotter place than we intended and for half an hour were under heavy shrapnel fire. I was curious to see how the youngster--for he was only fourteen-- would act. Finally he turned to me, his black eyes snapping with excitement. "Have I your permission to go a little nearer, monsieur?" he asked eagerly. "I won't be gone long. I only want to get a German helmet." It may have been the valour of ignorance which these broad-hatted, bare-kneed boys displayed, but it was the sort of valour which characterized every Belgian soldier. There was one youngster of thirteen who was attached to an officer of the staff and who was present at every battle of importance from the evacuation of Brussels to the fall of Antwerp. I remember seeing him during the retreat of the Belgians from Wesemael, curled up in the tonneau of a car and sleeping through all the turmoil and confusion. I felt like waking him up and saying sternly, "Look here, sonny, you'd better trot on home. Your mother will be worried to death about you." I believe that four Belgian boy scouts gave up their lives in the service of their country. Two were run down and killed by automobiles while on duty in Antwerp. Two others were, I understand, shot by German troops near Brussels while attempting to carry dispatches through the lines. One boy scout became so adept at this sort of work that he was regularly employed by the Government to carry messages through to its agents in Brussels. His exploits would provide material for a boy's book of adventure and, as a fitting conclusion, he was decorated by the King.

The last stand before Antwerp. Belgian levies being rushed to the front to dig trenches

Anyone who went to Belgium with hard-and-fast ideas as to social distinctions quickly had them shattered. The fact that a man wore a private's uniform and sat behind the steering-wheel of your car and respectfully touched his cap when you gave him an order did not imply that he had always been a chauffeur. Roos, who drove my car throughout my stay in Belgium, was the son of a Brussels millionaire, and at the beginning of hostilities had, as I think I have mentioned elsewhere, promptly presented his own powerful car to the

Government. The aristocracy of Belgium did not hang around the Ministry of War trying to obtain commissions. They simply donned privates' uniforms, and went into the firing-line. As a result of this wholehearted patriotism the ranks of the Belgian army were filled with men who were members of the most exclusive clubs and were welcome guests in the highest social circles in Europe. Almost any evening during the earlier part of the war a smooth-faced youth in the uniform of a private soldier could have been seen sitting amid a group of friends at dinner in the Hotel St. Antoine. When an officer entered the room he stood up and clicked his heels together and saluted. He was Prince Henri de Ligne, a member of one of the oldest and most distinguished families in Belgium and related to half the aristocracy of Europe. He, poor boy, was destined never again to follow the hounds or to lead a cotillion; he was killed near Herenthals with young Count de Villemont and Philippe de Zualart while engaged in a daring raid in an armoured motorcar into the German lines for the purpose of blowing up a bridge.

When, upon the occupation of Brussels by the Germans, the capital of Belgium was hastily transferred to Antwerp, considerable difficulty was experienced in finding suitable accommodation for the staffs of the various ministries, which were housed in any buildings which happened to be available at the time. Thus, the foreign relations of the nation were directed from a school-building in the Avenue du Commerce--the Foreign Minister, Monsieur Davignon, using as his Cabinet the room formerly used for lectures on physiology, the walls of which were still covered with blackboards and anatomical charts. The Grand Hotel was taken over by the Government for the accommodation of the Cabinet Ministers and their staffs, while the ministers of State and the members of the diplomatic corps were quartered at the St. Antoine. In fact, it used to be said in fun that if you got into difficulties with the police all you had to do was to get within the doors of the hotel, where you would be safe, for half of the ground floor was technically British soil, being occupied by the British Legation; a portion of the second floor was used by the Russian Legation; if you dashed into a certain bedroom you could claim Roumanian protection, and in another you were, theoretically, in Greece; while on the upper floor extra-territoriality was exercised by the Republic of China. Every evening all the ministers and diplomats met in the big rose-and-ivory dining-room--the white shirt- fronts of the men and the white shoulders of the women, with the uniforms of the Belgian officers and of the British, French and Russian military attaches, combining to form a wonderfully brilliant picture. Looking on that scene, it was hard to believe that by ascending to the roof of the hotel you could see the glare of burning villages and hear the boom of German cannon.

As the siege progressed and the German lines were drawn tighter, the military regulations governing life in Antwerp increased in severity. The local papers were not permitted to print any accounts of Belgian checks or reverses, and at one time the importation of English newspapers was suspended. Sealed letters were not accepted by the post office for any foreign countries save England, Russia and France, and even these were held four days before being forwarded. Telegrams were, of course, rigidly censored. The telephone service was suspended save for governmental purposes. At eight o'clock the trams stopped running. Save for a few ramshackle vehicles, drawn by decrepit horses, the cabs had disappeared from the streets. The city went spy-mad. If a man ordered Sauerkraut and sausage for lunch he instantly fell under suspicion. Scarcely a day passed without houses being raided and their occupants arrested on the charge of espionage. It was reported and generally believed that those whose guilt was proved were promptly executed outside the ramparts, but of this I have my doubts. The Belgians are too good-natured, too easy-going. It is probable, of course, that some spies were executed, but certainly not many.

One never stirred out of doors in Antwerp without one's papers, which had to be shown before one could gain admission to the post office, the telegraph bureau, the banks, the railway stations, or any other public buildings. There were several varieties of "papers." There was the plain passport which, beyond establishing your nationality, was not worth the paper it was written on. There was the permis de sejour, which was issued by the police to those who were able to prove that they had business which necessitated their remaining in the city. And finally, there was the much-prized laisser- passer which was issued by the military government and usually bore the photograph of the person to whom it was given, which proved an open sesame wherever shown, and which, I might add, was exceedingly difficult to obtain.

Only once did my laisser-passer fail me. During the final days of the siege, when the temper and endurance of the Belgian defenders were strained almost to the breaking-point, I motored out to witness the German assault on the forts near Willebroeck. With me were Captain Raymond Briggs of the United States army and Thompson. Before continuing to the front we took the precaution of stopping at division headquarters in Boom and asking if there was any objection to our proceeding; we were informed that there was none. We had not been on the firing-line half an hour, however, before two gendarmes came tearing up in a motor-car and informed us that we were under arrest and must return with them to Boom. At division headquarters we were interrogated by a staff major whose temper was as fiery as his hair. Thompson, as was his invariable custom, was smoking a very large and very black cigar.

"Take that cigar out of your mouth!" snapped the major in French. "How dare you smoke in my presence?"

"Sorry, major," said Thompson, grinning broadly, "but you'll have to talk American. I don't understand French."

"Stop smiling!" roared the now infuriated officer. "How dare you smile when I address you? This is no time for smiling, sir! This is a time of war!"

Though the major was reluctantly forced to admit that our papers were in order, we were nevertheless sent to staff headquarters in Antwerp guarded by two gendarmes, one of whom was the bearer of a dossier in which it was gravely recited that Captain Briggs and I had been arrested while in the company of a person calling himself Donald Thompson, who was charged by the chief of staff with having smiled and smoked a cigar in his presence. Needless to say, the whole opera-bouffe affair was promptly disavowed by the higher authorities.

I have mentioned the incident because it was the sole occasion on which I met with so much as a shadow of discourtesy from any Belgian, either soldier or civilian. I doubt if in any other country in the world in time of war, a foreigner would have been permitted to go where and when he pleased, as I was, and would have met with hospitality and kindness from every one.

The citizens of Antwerp hated the Germans with a deeper and more bitter hatred, if such a thing were possible, than the people of any other part of Belgium. This was due to the fact that in no foreign city where Germans dwelt and did business were they treated with such marked hospitality and consideration as in Antwerp. They had been given franchises and concessions and privileges of every description; they had been showered with honours and decorations; they were welcome guests on every occasion; city streets had been named after leading German residents; time and time again, both at private dinners and public banquets, they had asserted, wineglass in hand, their loyalty and devotion to the city which was their home. Yet, the moment opportunity offered, they did not scruple to betray it. In the cellar of the house belonging to one of the most prominent German residents the police found large stores of ammunition and hundreds of rifles and German uniforms. A German company had, as a result of criminal stupidity, been awarded the contract for wiring the forts defending the city--and when the need arose it was found that the wiring was all but worthless. A wealthy German had a magnificent country estate the gardens of which ran down to the moat of one of the outlying forts. One day he suggested to the military authorities that if they would permit him to obtain the necessary water from the moat, he would build a swimming-pool in his garden for the use of the soldiers. What appeared to be a generous offer was gladly accepted--but when the day of action came it was found that the moat had been drained dry. In the grounds of another country place were discovered concrete emplacements for the use of the German siege-guns. Thus the German residents repaid the hospitality of their adopted city.

When the war-cloud burst every German was promptly expelled from Antwerp. In a few cases the mob got out of hand and smashed the windows of some German saloons along the water-front, but no Germans were injured or mistreated. They were merely shipped, bag and baggage, across the frontier. That, in my opinion at least, is what should have been done with the entire civil population of Antwerp--provided, of course, that the Government intended to hold the city at all costs. The civilians seriously hampered the movements of the troops and thereby interfered with the defence; the presence of large numbers of women and children in the city during the bombardment unquestionably caused grave anxiety to the defenders and was probably one of the chief reasons for the evacuation taking place when it did; the masses of civilian fugitives who choked the roads in their mad flight from Antwerp were in large measure responsible for the capture of a considerable portion of the retreating Belgian army and for the fact that other bodies of troops were driven across the frontier and interned in Holland. So strongly was the belief that Antwerp was impregnable implanted in every Belgian's mind, however, that up to the very last not one citizen in a thousand would admit that there was a possibility that it could be taken. The army did not believe that it could be taken. The General Staff did not believe that it could be taken. They were destined to have a rude and sad awakening.

The effect of one of the bombs dropped from the Zeppelin.
The thick walls of the houses were perforated as easily as one
jabs a pencil through a sheet of paper

Steel bridge at Termonde destroyed by shell fire

Another bridge at Termonde destroyed by the Germans

III. The Death In The Air

At eleven minutes past one o'clock on the morning of August 25 death came to Antwerp out of the air. Some one had sent a bundle of English and American newspapers to my room in the Hotel St. Antoine and I had spent the evening reading them, so that the bells of the cathedral had already chimed one o'clock when I switched off my light and opened the window. As I did so my attention was attracted by a curious humming overhead, like a million bumblebees. I leaned far out of the window, and as I did so an indistinct mass, which gradually resolved itself into something resembling a gigantic black cigar, became plainly apparent against the purple-velvet sky. I am not good at estimating altitudes, but I should say that when I first caught sight of it it was not more than a thousand feet above my head--and my room was on the top floor of the hotel, remember. As it drew nearer the noise, which had at first reminded me of a swarm of angry bees, grew louder, until it sounded like an automobile with the muffler open. Despite the darkness there was no doubting what it was. It was a German Zeppelin.

Even as I looked something resembling a falling star curved across the sky. An instant later came a rending, shattering crash that shook the hotel to its foundations, the walls of my room rocked and reeled, about me, and for a breathless moment I thought that the building was going to collapse. Perhaps thirty seconds later came another splitting explosion, and another, and then another--ten in all--each, thank Heaven, a little farther removed. It was all so sudden, so utterly unexpected, that it must have been quite a minute before I realized that the monstrous thing hovering in the darkness overhead was one of the dirigibles of which we had read and talked so much, and that it was actually raining death upon the sleeping city from the sky. I suppose it was blind instinct that caused me to run to the door and down the corridor with the idea of getting into the street, never stopping to reason, of course, that there was no protection in the street from Zeppelins. But before I had gone a dozen paces I had my nerves once more in hand. "Perhaps it isn't a Zeppelin, after all," I argued to myself. "I may have been dreaming. And how perfectly ridiculous I should look if I were to dash downstairs in my pyjamas and find that nothing had happened. At least I'll go back and put some clothes on." And I did. No fireman, responding to a night alarm, ever dressed quicker. As I ran through the corridors the doors of bedrooms opened and sleepy-eyed, tousle-headed diplomatists and Government officials called after me to ask if the Germans were bombarding the city.

"They are," I answered, without stopping. There was no time to explain that for the first time in history a city was being bombarded from the air.

I found the lobby rapidly filling with scantily clad guests, whose teeth were visibly chattering. Guided by the hotel manager and accompanied by half a dozen members of the diplomatic corps in pyjamas, I raced upstairs to a sort of observatory on the hotel roof. I remember that one attache of the British Legation, ordinarily a most dignified person, had on some sort of a night-robe of purple silk and that when he started to climb the iron ladder of the fire-escape he looked for all the world like a burglarious suffragette.

By the time we reached the roof of the hotel Belgian high-angle and machine-guns were stabbing the darkness with spurts of flame, the troops of the garrison were blazing away with rifles, and the gendarmes in the streets were shooting wildly with their revolvers: the noise was deafening. Oblivious of the consternation and confusion it had caused, the Zeppelin, after letting fall a final bomb, slowly rose and disappeared in the upper darkness.

The destruction wrought by the German projectiles was almost incredible. The first shell, which I had seen fall, struck a building in the Rue de la Bourse, barely two hundred yards in a straight line from my window. A hole was not merely blown through the roof, as would have been the case with a shell from a field-gun, but the three upper stories simply crumbled, disintegrated, came crashing down in an avalanche of brick and stone and plaster, as though a Titan had hit it with a sledge-hammer. Another shell struck in the middle of the Poids Public, or public weighing-place, which is about the size of Russell Square in London. It blew a hole in the cobblestone- pavement large enough to bury a horse in; one policeman on duty at the far end of the square was instantly killed and another had both legs blown off. But this was not all nor nearly all. Six people sleeping in houses fronting on the square were killed in their beds and a dozen others were more or less seriously wounded. Every building facing on the square was either wholly or partially demolished, the steel splinters of the projectile tearing their way through the thick brick-walls as easily as a lead-pencil is jabbed through a sheet of paper. And, as a result of the terrific concussion, every house within a hundred yards of the square in every direction had its windows broken. On no battlefield have I ever seen so horrible a sight as that which turned me weak and nauseated when I entered one of the shattered houses and made my way, over heaps of fallen debris, to a room where a young woman had been sleeping. She had literally been blown to fragments. The floor, the walls, the ceiling, were splotched with--well, it's enough to say that that woman's remains could only have been collected with a shovel. In saying this, I am not speaking flippantly either. I have dwelt upon these details, revolting as they are, because I wish to drive home the fact that the only victims of this air-raid on Antwerp were innocent non-combatants.

Another shell struck the roof of a physician's house in the fashionable Rue des Escrimeurs, killing two maids who were sleeping in a room on the upper floor. A shell fell in a garden in the Rue von Bary, terribly wounding a man and his wife. A little child was mangled by a shell which struck a house in the Rue de la Justice. Another shell fell in the barracks in the Rue Falcon, killing one inmate and wounding two others. By a fortunate coincidence the regiment which had been quartered in the barracks had left for the front on the previous day. A woman who was awakened by the first explosion and leaned from her window to see what was happening had her head blown off. In all ten people were killed, six of whom were women, and upwards of forty wounded, two of them so terribly that they afterwards died. There is very little doubt that a deliberate attempt was made to kill the royal family, the General Staff and the members of the Government, one shell bursting within a hundred yards of the royal palace, where the King and Queen were sleeping, and another within two hundred yards of staff headquarters and the Hotel St. Antoine.

As a result of this night of horror, Antwerp, to use an inelegant but descriptive expression, developed a violent case of the jim-jams. The next night and every night thereafter until the Germans came in and took the city, she thought she saw things; not green rats and pink snakes, but large, sausage-shaped balloons with bombs dropping from them. The military authorities--for the city was under martial law--screwed down the lid so tight that even the most rabid prohibitionists and social reformers murmured. As a result of the precautionary measures which were taken, Antwerp, with its four hundred thousand inhabitants, became about as cheerful a place of residence as a country cemetery on a rainy evening. At eight o'clock every street light was turned off, every shop and restaurant and cafe closed, every window darkened. If a light was seen in a window after eight o'clock the person who occupied that room was in grave danger of being arrested for signalling to the enemy. My room, which was on the third floor of the hotel, was so situated that its windows could not be seen from the street, and hence I was not as particular about lowering the shades as I should have been. The second night after the Zeppelin raid the manager came bursting into my room. "Quick, Mr. Powell," he called, excitedly, "pull down your shade. The observers in the cathedral tower have just sent word that your windows are lighted and the police are downstairs to find out what it means."

The darkness of London and Paris was a joke beside the darkness of Antwerp. It was so dark in the narrow, winding streets, bordered by ancient houses, that when, as was my custom, I went to the telegraph office with my dispatches after dinner, I had to feel my way with a cane, like a blind man. To make conditions more intolerable, if such a thing were possible, cordons of sentries were thrown around those buildings under whose roofs the members of the Government slept, so that if one returned after nightfall he was greeted by a harsh command to halt, and a sentry held a rifle- muzzle against his breast while another sentry, by means of a dark lantern, scrutinized his papers. Save for the sentries, the streets were deserted, for, as the places of amusement and the eating- places and drinking-places were closed, there was no place for the people to go except to bed. I was reminded of the man who told his wife that he came home because all the other places were closed.

I have heard it said that Antwerp was indifferent to its fate, but it made no such impression on me. Never have I lived in such an atmosphere of gloom and depression. Except around the St. Antoine at the lunch and dinner-hours and in the cafes just before nightfall did one see anything which was even a second cousin to jollity. The people did not smile. They went about with grave and anxious faces. In fact, outside of the places I have mentioned, one rarely heard a laugh. The people who sat at the round iron tables on the sidewalks in front of the cafes drinking their light wines and beer --no spirits were permitted to be sold--sat in silence and with solemn faces. God knows, there was little enough for them to smile about. Their nation was being slowly strangled. Three-quarters of its soil was under the heel of the invader. An alien flag, a hated flag, flew over their capital. Their King and their Government were fugitives, moving from place to place as a vagrant moves on at the approach of a policeman. Men who, a month before, were prosperous shopkeepers and tradesmen were virtual bankrupts, not knowing where the next hundred-franc note was coming from. Other men had seen their little flower-surrounded homes in the suburbs razed to the ground that an approaching enemy might find no cover. Though the shops were open, they had no customers for the people had no money, or, if they had money they were hoarding it against the days when they might be homeless fugitives. No, there was not very much to smile about in Antwerp.

There were amusing incidents, of course. If one recognizes humour when he sees it he can find it in almost any situation. After the first Zeppelin attack the management of the St. Antoine fitted up bedrooms in the cellars.

A century or more ago the St. Antoine was not a hotel but a monastery, and its cellars are all that the cellars of a monastery ought to be--thick-walled and damp and musty. Yet these subterranean suites were in as great demand among the diplomatists as are tables in the palm-room of the Savoy during the season. From my bedroom window, which overlooked the court, I could see apprehensive guests cautiously emerging from their cellar chambers in the early morning. It reminded me of woodchucks coming out of their holes.

As the siege progressed and the German guns were pushed nearer to the city, those who lived in what might be termed "conspicuous" localities began to seek other quarters.

"I'm going to change hotels to-day," I heard a man remark to a friend.

"Why?" inquired the other.

"Because I am within thirty yards of the cathedral," was the answer. The towering spire of the famous cathedral is, you must understand, the most conspicuous thing in Antwerp--on clear days you can see it from twenty miles away--and to live in its immediate vicinity during a bombardment of the city was equivalent to taking shelter under the only tree in a field during a heavy thunderstorm.

Two days before the bombardment began there was a meeting of the American residents--such of them as still remained in the city--at the leading club. About a dozen of us in all sat down to dinner. The purpose of the gathering was to discuss the attitude which the Americans should adopt towards the German officers, for it was known that the fall of the city was imminent. I remember that the sense of the meeting was that we should treat the helmeted intruders with frigid politeness--I think that was the term--which, translated, meant that we were not to offer them cigars and buy them drinks. Of the twelve of us who sat around the table that night, there are only two--Mr. Manly Whedbee and myself--who remained to witness the German occupation.

That the precautions taken against Zeppelins were by no means overdone was proved by the total failure of the second aerial raid on Antwerp, in the latter part of September, when a dirigible again sailed over the city under cover of darkness. Owing to the total absence of street-lights, however, the dirigible's crew were evidently unable to get their bearings, for the half-dozen bombs that they discharged fell in the outskirts of the city without causing any loss of life or doing any serious damage. This time, moreover, the Belgians were quite prepared--the fire of their "sky artillery," guided by searchlights, making things exceedingly uncomfortable for the Germans.

I have heard it stated by Belgian officers and others that the bombs were dropped from the dirigibles by an ingenious arrangement which made the airship itself comparatively safe from harm and at the same time rendered the aim of its bombmen much more accurate. According to them, the dirigible comes to a stop--or as near a stop as possible--above the city or fortification which it wishes to attack, at a height out of range of either artillery or rifle-fire. Then, by means of a steel cable a thousand feet or more in length, it lowers a small wire cage just large enough to contain a man and a supply of bombs, this cage being sufficiently armoured so that it is proof against rifle-bullets. At the same time it affords so tiny a mark that the chances of its being hit by artillery-fire are insignificant. If it should be struck, moreover, the airship itself would still be unharmed and only one man would be lost, and when he fell his supply of bombs would fall with him. The Zeppelin, presumably equipped with at least two cages and cables, might at once lower another bomb-thrower. I do not pretend to say whether this ingenious contrivance is used by the Germans. Certainly the Zeppelin which I saw in action had nothing of the kind, nor did it drop its projectiles promiscuously, as one would drop a stone, but apparently discharged them from a bomb-tube.

Though the Zeppelin raids proved wholly ineffective, so far as their effect on troops and fortifications were concerned, the German aviators introduced some novel tricks in aerial warfare which were as practical as they were ingenious. During the battle of Vilvorde, for example, and throughout the attacks on the Antwerp forts, German dirigibles hovered at a safe height over the Belgian positions and directed the fire of the German gunners with remarkable success. The aerial observers watched, through powerful glasses, the effect of the German shells and then, by means of a large disc which was swung at the end of a line and could be raised or lowered at will, signalled as need be in code "higher--lower--right--left" and thus guided the gunners--who were, of course, unable to see their mark or the effect of their fire--until almost every shot was a hit. At Vilvorde, as a result of this aerial fire-control system, I saw the German artillery, posted out of sight behind a railway embankment, get the range of a retreating column of Belgian infantry and with a dozen well-placed shots practically wipe it out of existence. So perfect was the German system of observation and fire control during the final attack on the Antwerp defences that whenever the Belgians or British moved a regiment or a battery the aerial observers instantly detected it and a perfect storm of shells was directed against the new position.

Throughout the operations around Antwerp, the Taubes, as the German aeroplanes are called because of their fancied resemblance to a dove, repeatedly performed daring feats of reconnaissance. On one occasion, while I was with the General Staff at Lierre, one of these German Taubes sailed directly over the Hotel de Ville, which was being used as staff headquarters. It so happened that King Albert was standing in the street, smoking one of the seven-for-a-franc Belgian cigars to which he was partial.

"The Germans call it a dove, eh?" remarked the King, as he looked up at the passing aircraft. "Well, it looks to me more like a hawk."

A few days before the fall of Antwerp a Taube flew over the city in the early afternoon, dropping thousands of proclamations printed in both French and Flemish and signed by the commander of the investing forces, pointing out to the inhabitants the futility of resistance, asserting that in fighting Germany they were playing Russia's game, and urging them to lay down their arms. The aeroplane was greeted by a storm of shrapnel from the high-angle guns mounted on the fortifications, the only effect of which, however, was to kill two unoffending citizens who were standing in the streets and were struck by the fragments of the falling shells.

Most people seem to have the impression that it is as easy for an aviator to see what is happening on the ground beneath him as though he were looking down from the roof of a high building. Under ordinary conditions, when one can skim above the surface of the earth at a height of a few hundred feet, this is quite true, but it is quite a different matter when one is flying above hostile troops who are blazing away at him with rifles and machine-guns. During reconnaissance work the airmen generally are compelled to ascend to an altitude of a mile or a mile and a quarter, which makes observation extremely difficult, as small objects, even with the aid of the strongest glasses, assume unfamiliar shapes and become fore- shortened. If, in order to obtain a better view, they venture to fly at a lower height, they are likely to be greeted by a hail of rifle fire from soldiers in the trenches. The Belgian aviators with whom I talked assured me that they feared rifle fire more than bursting shrapnel, as the fire of a regiment, when concentrated even on so elusive an object as an aeroplane, proves far more deadly than shells.

The Belgians made more use than any other nation of motor-cars. When war was declared one of the first steps taken by the military authorities was to commandeer every motor-car, every motor-cycle and every litre of petrol in the kingdom. As a result they depended almost entirely upon motor-driven vehicles for their military transport, which was, I might add, extremely efficient. In fact, we could always tell when we were approaching the front by the amazing number of motor-cars which lined the roads for miles in the rear of each division.

Anything that had four wheels and a motor to drive them--diminutive American run-abouts, slim, low-hung racing cars, luxurious limousines with coronets painted on the panels, delivery-cars bearing the names of shops in Antwerp and Ghent and Brussels, lumbering motor-trucks, hotel omnibuses--all met the same fate, which consisted in being daubed with elephant-grey paint, labelled "S.M." (Service Militaire) in staring white letters, and started for the front, usually in charge of a wholly inexperienced driver. It made an automobile lover groan to see the way some of those cars were treated. But they did the business. They averaged something like twelve miles an hour--which is remarkable time for army transport-- and, strangely enough, very few of them broke down. If they did there was always an automobile des reparations promptly on hand to repair the damage. Before the war began the Belgian army had no army transport worthy of the name; before the forts at Liege had been silenced it had as efficient a one as any nation in Europe.

The headquarters of the motor-car branch of the army was at the Pare des Automobiles Militaires, on the Red Star quays in Antwerp. Here several hundred cars were always kept in reserve, and here was collected an enormous store of automobile supplies and sundries. The scene under the long, low sheds, with their corrugated-iron roofs, always reminded me of the Automobile Show at Olympia. After a car had once been placed at your disposal by the Government, getting supplies for it was merely a question of signing bons. Obtaining extra equipment for my car was Roos' chief amusement. Tyres, tools, spare parts, horns, lamps, trunks--all you had to do was to scrawl your name at the foot of a printed form and they were promptly handed over. When I first went to Belgium I was given a sixty horse-power touring car, and when the weather turned unpleasant I asked for and was given a limousine that was big enough to sleep in, and when I found this too clumsy, the commandant of the Parc des Automobiles obligingly exchanged it for a ninety horse-power berline. They were most accommodating, those Belgians. I am sorry to say that my berline, which was the envy of every one in Antwerp, was eventually captured by the Germans.

Belgian armoured motor-car going into action near Ghent. (Note the barricade in the background)

Belgian armoured motor-car firing across a dyke near Boom

Though both the French and the Germans had for a number of years been experimenting with armoured cars of various patterns, the Belgians, who had never before given the subject serious consideration, were the first to evolve and to send into action a really practical vehicle of this description. The earlier armoured cars used by the Belgians were built at the great Minerva factory in Antwerp and consisted of a circular turret, high enough so that only the head and shoulders of the man operating the machine-gun were exposed, covered with half-inch steel plates and mounted on an ordinary chassis. After the disastrous affair near Herenthals, in which Prince Henri de Ligne was mortally wounded while engaged in a raid into the German lines for the purpose of blowing up bridges, it was seen that the crew of the auto-mitrailleuses, as the armoured cars were called, was insufficiently protected, and, to remedy this, a movable steel dome, with an opening for the muzzle of the machine-gun, was superimposed on the turret. These grim vehicles, which jeered at bullets, and were proof even against shrapnel, quickly became a nightmare to the Germans. Driven by the most reckless racing drivers in Belgium, manned by crews of dare-devil youngsters, and armed with machine-guns which poured out lead at the rate of a thousand shots a minute, these wheeled fortresses would tear at will into the German lines, cut up an outpost or wipe out a cavalry patrol, dynamite a bridge or a tunnel or a culvert, and be back in the Belgian lines again almost before the enemy realized what had happened.

The Belgian firing-line near Malines

I witnessed an example of the cool daring of these mitrailleuse drivers during the fighting around Malines. Standing on a railway embankment, I was watching the withdrawal under heavy fire of the last Belgian troops, when an armoured car, the lean muzzle of its machine-gun peering from its turret, tore past me at fifty miles an hour, spitting a murderous spray of lead as it bore down on the advancing Germans. But when within a few hundred yards of the German line the car slackened speed and stopped. Its petrol was exhausted. Instantly one of the crew was out in the road and, under cover of the fire from the machine-gun, began to refill the tank. Though bullets were kicking up spurts of dust in the road or ping- pinging against the steel turret he would not be hurried. I, who was watching the scene through my field-glasses, was much more excited than he was. Then, when the tank was filled, the car refused to back! It was a big machine and the narrow road was bordered on either side by deep ditches, but by a miracle the driver was able-- and just able--to turn the car round. Though by this time the German gunners had the range and shrapnel was bursting all about him, he was as cool as though he were turning a limousine in the width of Piccadilly. As the car straightened out for its retreat, the Belgians gave the Germans a jeering screech from their horn, and a parting blast of lead from their machine-gun and went racing Antwerpwards.

A chapel of the Cathedral of Malines, wrecked by German shells.

It is, by the way, a curious and interesting fact that the machine-gun used in both the Belgian and Russian armoured cars, and which is one of the most effective weapons produced by the war, was repeatedly offered to the American War Department by its inventor, Major Isaac Newton Lewis, of the United States army, and was as repeatedly rejected by the officials at Washington. At last, in despair of receiving recognition in his own country, he sold it to Russia and Belgium. The Lewis gun, which is air-cooled and weighs only twenty-nine pounds--less than half the weight of a soldier's equipment--fires a thousand shots a minute. In the fighting around Sempst I saw trees as large round as a man's thigh literally cut down by the stream of lead from these weapons.

The inventor of the Lewis gun was not the only American who played an inconspicuous but none the less important part in the War of Nations. A certain American corporation doing business in Belgium placed its huge Antwerp plant and the services of its corps of skilled engineers at the service of the Government, though I might add that this fact was kept carefully concealed, being known to only a handful of the higher Belgian officials. This concern made shells and other ammunition for the Belgian army; it furnished aeroplanes and machine-guns; it constructed miles of barbed-wire entanglements and connected those entanglements with the city lighting system; one of its officers went on a secret mission to England and brought back with him a supply of cordite, not to mention six large-calibre guns which he smuggled through Dutch territorial waters hidden in the steamer's coal bunkers. And, as though all this were not enough, the Belgian Government confided to this foreign corporation the minting of the national currency. For obvious reasons I am not at liberty to mention the name of this concern, though it is known to practically every person in the United States, each month cheques being sent to the parent concern by eight hundred thousand people in New York alone.

Incidentally it publishes the most widely read volume in the world. I wish that I might tell you the name of this concern. Upon second thought, I think I will. It is the American Bell Telephone Company.

The Invaders

IV. Under The German Eagle

When, upon the approach of the Germans to Brussels, the Government and the members of the Diplomatic Corps fled to Antwerp, the American Minister, Mr. Brand Whitlock, did not accompany them. In view of the peculiar position occupied by the United States as the only Great Power not involved in hostilities, he felt, and, as it proved, quite rightly, that he could be of more service to Belgium and to Brussels and to the cause of humanity in general by remaining behind. There remained with him the secretary of legation, Mr. Hugh S. Gibson. Mr. Whitlock's reasons for remaining in Brussels were twofold. In the first place, there were a large number of English and Americans, both residents and tourists, who had been either unable or unwilling to leave the city, and who, he felt, were entitled to diplomatic protection. Secondly, the behaviour of the German troops in other Belgian cities had aroused grave fears of what would happen when they entered Brussels, and it was generally felt that the presence of the American Minister might deter them from committing the excesses and outrages which up to that time had characterized their advance. It was no secret that Germany was desperately anxious to curry favour with the United States, and it was scarcely likely, therefore, that houses would be sacked and burnt, civilians executed and women violated under the disapproving eyes of the American representative. This surmise proved to be well founded. The Germans did not want Mr. Whitlock in Brussels, and nothing would have pleased them better than to have had him depart and leave them to their own devices, but, so long as he blandly ignored their hints that his room was preferable to his company and persisted in sitting tight, they submitted to his surveillance with the best grace possible and behaved themselves as punctiliously as a dog that has been permitted to come into a parlour. After the civil administration had been established, however, and Belgium had become, in theory at least, a German province, Mr. Whitlock was told quite plainly that the kingdom to which he was accredited had ceased to exist as an independent nation, and that Anglo-American affairs in Belgium could henceforward be entrusted to the American Ambassador at Berlin. But Mr. .Whitlock, who had received his training in shirt-sleeve diplomacy as Socialist Mayor of Toledo, Ohio, was as impervious to German suggestions as he had been to the threats and pleadings of party politicians, and told Baron von der Golz, the German Governor, politely but quite firmly, that he did not take his orders from Berlin but from Washington. "Gott in Himmel!" exclaimed the Germans, shrugging their shoulders despairingly, "what is to be done with such a man?"

Before the Germans had been in occupation of Brussels a fortnight the question of food for the poorer classes became a serious and pressing problem. The German armies, in their onset toward the west, had swept the Belgian country-side bare; the products of the farms and gardens in the immediate vicinity of the city had been commandeered for the use of the garrison, and the spectre of starvation was already beginning to cast its dread shadow over Brussels. Mr. Whitlock acted with promptness and decision. He sent Americans, who had volunteered their services, to Holland to purchase food-stuffs, and at the same time informed the German commander that he expected these food-stuffs to be admitted without hindrance. The German replied that he could not comply with this request without first communicating with his Imperial master, whereupon he was told, in effect, that the American Government would consider him personally responsible if the food- stuffs were delayed or diverted for military use and a famine ensued in consequence. The firmness of Mr. Whitlock's attitude had its effect, for at seven o'clock the next morning he received word that his wishes would be complied with. As a result of the German occupation, Brussels, with its six hundred thousand inhabitants, was as completely cut off from communication with the outside world as though it were on an island in the South Pacific. The postal, telegraph and telephone services were suspended; the railways were blocked with troop trains moving westward; the roads were filled from ditch to ditch with troops and transport wagons; and so tightly were the lines drawn between that portion of Belgium occupied by the Germans and that still held by the Belgians, that those daring souls who attempted to slip through the cordons of sentries did so at peril of their lives. It sounds almost incredible that a great city could be so effectually isolated, yet so it was. Even the Cabinet Ministers and other officials who had accompanied the Government in its flight to Antwerp were unable to learn what had befallen the families which they had in many cases left behind them.

After nearly three weeks had passed without word from the American Legation, the Department of State cabled the American Consul-General at Antwerp that some means of communicating with Mr. Whitlock must be found. Happening to be in the Consulate when the message was received, I placed my services and my car at the disposal of the Consul-General, who promptly accepted them. Upon learning of my proposed jaunt into the enemy's lines, a friend, Mr. M. Manly Whedbee, the director of the Belgian branch of the British- American Tobacco Company, offered to accompany me, and as he is as cool-headed and courageous and companionable as anyone I know, and as he knew as much about driving the car as I did--for it was obviously impossible to take my Belgian driver--I was only too glad to have him with me. It was, indeed, due to Mr. Whedbee's foresight in taking along a huge quantity of cigarettes for distribution among the soldiers, that we were able to escape from Brussels. But more of that episode hereafter.

When the Consul-General asked General Dufour, the military governor of Antwerp, to issue us a safe conduct through the Belgian lines, that gruff old soldier at first refused flatly, asserting that as the German outposts had been firing on cars bearing the Red Cross flag, there was no assurance that they would respect one bearing the Stars and Stripes. The urgency of the matter being explained to him, however, he reluctantly issued the necessary laisser-passer, though intimating quite plainly that our mission would probably end in providing "more work for the undertaker, another little job for the casket-maker," and that he washed his hands of all responsibility for our fate. But by two American flags mounted on the windshield, and the explanatory legends "Service Consulaire des Etats-Unis d'Amerique" and "Amerikanischer Consular dienst" painted in staring letters on the hood, we hoped to make it quite clear to Germans and Belgians alike that we were protected by the international game-laws so far as shooting us was concerned.

Now the disappointing thing about our trip was that we didn't encounter any Uhlans. Every one had warned us so repeatedly about Uhlans that we fully expected to find them, with their pennoned lances and their square-topped schapskas, lurking behind every hedge, and when they did not come spurring out to intercept us we were greatly disappointed. It was like making a journey to the polar regions and seeing no Esquimaux. The smart young cavalry officer who bade us good-bye at the Belgian outposts, warned us to keep our eyes open for them and said, rather mournfully, I thought, that he only hoped they would give us time to explain who we were before they opened fire on us. "They are such hasty fellows, these Uhlans," said he, "always shooting first and making inquiries afterward." As a matter of fact, the only Uhlan we saw on the entire trip was riding about Brussels in a cab, smoking a large porcelain pipe and with his spurred boots resting comfortably on the cushions.

One of the German field-guns

Though we crept along as circumspectly as a motorist who knows that he is being trailed by a motorcycle policeman, peering behind farmhouses and hedges and into the depths of thickets and expecting any moment to hear a gruff command, emphasized by the bang of a carbine, it was not until we were at the very outskirts of Aerschot that we encountered the Germans. There were a hundred of them, so cleverly ambushed behind a hedge that we would never have suspected their presence had we not caught the glint of sunlight on their rifle-barrels. We should not have gotten much nearer, in any event, for they had a wire neatly strung across the road at just the right height to take us under the chins. When we were within a hundred yards of the hedge an officer in a trailing grey cloak stepped into the middle of the road and held up his hand.

German soldiers being fed from a field kitchen

German pom-poms going into action

"Halt!"

I jammed on the brakes so suddenly that we nearly went through the windshield.

"Get out of the automobile and stand well away from it," the officer commanded in German. We got out very promptly.

"One of you advance alone, with his hands up."

I advanced alone, but not with my hands up. It is such an undignified position. I had that shivery feeling chasing up and down my spine which came from knowing that I was covered by a hundred rifles, and that if I made a move which seemed suspicious to the men behind those rifles, they would instantly transform me into a sieve.

"Are you English?" the officer demanded, none too pleasantly.

"No, American," said I.

"Oh, that's all right," said he, his manner instantly thawing. "I know America well," he continued, "Atlantic City and Asbury Park and Niagara Falls and Coney Island. I have seen all of your famous places."

German infantry on the march in Belgium. " The men had the pink cheeks of athletes and walked with the buoyancy of perfect health "

Imagine, if you please, standing in the middle of a Belgian highway, surrounded by German soldiers who looked as though they would rather shoot you than not, discussing the relative merits of the hotels at Atlantic City and which had the best dining-car service, the Pennsylvania or the New York Central!

I learned from the officer, who proved to be an exceedingly agreeable fellow, that had we advanced ten feet further after the command to halt was given, we should probably have been planted in graves dug in a nearby potato field, as only an hour before our arrival a Belgian mitrailleuse car had torn down the road with its machine-gun squirting a stream of lead, and had smashed straight through the German line, killing three men and wounding a dozen others. They were burying them when we appeared. When our big grey machine hove in sight they not unnaturally took us for another armoured car and prepared to give us a warm reception. It was a lucky thing for us that our brakes worked quickly.

Mr. Powell (in car) amid the ruins of Aerschot

We were the first foreigners to see Aerschot, or rather what was left of Aerschot after it had been sacked and burned by the Germans. A few days before Aerschot had been a prosperous and happy town of ten thousand people. When we saw it it was but a heap of smoking ruins, garrisoned by a battalion of German soldiers, and with its population consisting of half a hundred white-faced women. In many parts of the world I have seen many terrible and revolting things, but nothing so ghastly, so horrifying as Aerschot. Quite two- thirds of the houses had been burned and showed unmistakable signs of having been sacked by a maddened soldiery before they were burned. Everywhere were the ghastly evidences. Doors had been smashed in with rifle-butts and boot-heels; windows had been broken; furniture had been wantonly destroyed; pictures had been torn from the walls; mattresses had been ripped open with bayonets in search of valuables; drawers had been emptied upon the floors; the outer walls of the houses were spattered with blood and pock- marked with bullets; the sidewalks were slippery with broken wine- bottles; the streets were strewn with women's clothing. It needed no one to tell us the details of that orgy of blood and lust. The story was so plainly written that anyone could read it.

Before the Germans came Aerschot was as smiling, prosperous a place as you would find anywhere ; this is what it looked like when they left

For a mile we drove the car slowly between the blackened walls of fire-gutted buildings. This was no accidental conflagration, mind you, for scattered here and there were houses which stood undamaged and in every such case there was scrawled with chalk upon their doors "Gute Leute. Nicht zu plundern." (Good people. Do not plunder.)

The Germans went about the work of house-burning as systematically as they did everything else. They had various devices for starting conflagrations, all of them effective. At Aerschot and Louvain they broke the windows of the houses and threw in sticks which had been soaked in oil and dipped in sulphur. Elsewhere they used tiny, black tablets, about the size of cough lozenges, made of some highly inflammable composition, to which they touched a match. At Termonde, which they destroyed in spite of the fact that the inhabitants had evacuated the city before their arrival, they used a motor-car equipped with a large tank for petrol, a pump, a hose, and a spraying-nozzle. The car was run slowly through the streets, one soldier working the pump and another spraying the fronts of the houses. Then they set fire to them. Oh, yes, they were very methodical about it all, those Germans.

Despite the scowls of the soldiers, I attempted to talk with some of the women huddled in front of a bakery waiting for a distribution of bread, but the poor creatures were too terror-stricken to do more than stare at us with wide, beseeching eyes. Those eyes will always haunt me. I wonder if they do not sometimes haunt the Germans. But a little episode that occurred as we were leaving the city did more than anything else to bring home the horror of it all. We passed a little girl of nine or ten and I stopped the car to ask the way. Instantly she held both hands above her head and began to scream for mercy. When we had given her some chocolate and money, and had assured her that we were not Germans, but Americans and friends, she ran like a frightened deer. That little child, with her fright-wide eyes and her hands raised in supplication, was in herself a terrible indictment of the Germans.

This is what the Germans did to Aerschot

There are, as might be expected, two versions of the happenings which precipitated that night of horrors in Aerschot. The German version--I had it from the German commander himself--is to the effect that after the German troops had entered Aerschot, the Chief of Staff and some of the officers were asked to dinner by the burgomaster. While they were seated at the table the son of the burgomaster, a boy of fifteen, entered the room with a revolver and killed the Chief of Staff, whereupon, as though at a prearranged signal, the townspeople opened fire from their windows upon the troops. What followed--the execution of the burgomaster, his son, and several score of the leading townsmen, the giving over of the women to a lust-mad soldiery, the sacking of the houses, and the final burning of the town--was the punishment which would always be meted out to towns whose inhabitants attacked German soldiers.

Now, up to a certain point the Belgian version agrees with the German. It is admitted that the Germans entered the town peaceably enough, that the German Chief of Staff and other officers accepted the hospitality of the burgomaster, and that, while they were at dinner, the burgomaster's son entered the room and shot the Chief of Staff dead with a revolver. But--and this is the point to which the German story makes no allusion--the boy killed the Chief of Staff in defence of his sister's honour. It is claimed that toward the end of the meal the German officer, inflamed with wine, informed the burgomaster that he intended to pass the night with his young and beautiful daughter, whereupon the girl's brother quietly slipped from the room and, returning a moment later, put a sudden end to the German's career with an automatic. What the real truth is I do not know. Perhaps no one knows. The Germans did not leave many eye-witnesses to tell the story of what happened. Piecing together the stories told by those who did survive that night of horror, we know that scores of the townspeople were shot down in cold blood and that, when the firing squads could not do the work of slaughter fast enough, the victims were lined up and a machine-gun was turned upon them. We know that young girls were dragged from their homes and stripped naked and violated by soldiers--many soldiers--in the public square in the presence of officers. We know that both men and women were unspeakably mutilated, that children were bayoneted, that dwellings were ransacked and looted, and that finally, as though to destroy the evidences of their horrid work, soldiers went from house to house with torches, methodically setting fire to them.

It was with a feeling of repulsion amounting almost to nausea that we left what had once been Aerschot behind us. The road leading to Louvain was alive with soldiery, and we were halted every few minutes by German patrols. Had not the commanding officer in Aerschot detailed two bicyclists to accompany us I doubt if we should have gotten through. Whedbee had had the happy idea of bringing along a thousand packets of cigarettes--the tonneau of the car was literally filled with them--and we tossed a packet to every German soldier that we saw. You could have followed our trail for thirty miles by the cigarettes we left behind us. As it turned out, they were the means of saving us from being detained within the German lines.

The Ninth German Army crossing the Belgian frontier into France. Far as the eye could see the column of marching men stretched like a monstrous grey snake across the countryside

Thanks to our American flags, to the nature of our mission, and to our wholesale distribution of cigarettes, we were passed from outpost to outpost and from regimental headquarters to regimental headquarters until we reached Louvain. Here we came upon another scene of destruction and desolation. Nearly half the city was in ashes. Most of the principal streets were impassable from fallen masonry. The splendid avenues and boulevards were lined on either side by the charred skeletons of what had once been handsome buildings. The fronts of many of the houses were smeared with crimson stains. In comparison to its size, the Germans had wrought more widespread destruction in Louvain than did the earthquake and fire combined in San Francisco. The looting had evidently been unrestrained. The roads for miles in either direction were littered with furniture and bedding and clothing. Such articles as the soldiers could not carry away they wantonly destroyed. Hangings had been torn down, pictures on the walls had been smashed, the contents of drawers and trunks had been emptied into the streets, literally everything breakable had been broken. This is not from hearsay, remember; I saw it with my own eyes. And the amazing feature of it all was that among the Germans there seemed to be no feeling of regret, no sense of shame. Officers in immaculate uniforms strolled about among the ruins, chatting and laughing and smoking. At one place a magnificent mahogany dining-table had been dragged into the middle of the road and about it, sprawled in carved and tapestry-covered chairs, a dozen German infantrymen were drinking beer.

Just as there are two versions of the destruction of Aerschot, so there are two versions, though in this case widely different, of the events which led up to the destruction of Louvain. It should be borne in mind, to begin with, that Louvain was not destroyed by bombardment or in the heat of battle, for the Germans had entered it unopposed, and had been in undisputed possession for several days. The Germans assert that a conspiracy, fomented by the burgomaster, the priests and many of the leading citizens, existed among the townspeople, who planned to suddenly fall upon and exterminate the garrison. They claim that, in pursuance of this plan, on the night of August 26, the inhabitants opened a murderous fire upon the unsuspecting troops from house-tops, doors and windows; that a fierce street battle ensued, in which a number of women and children were unfortunately killed by stray bullets; and that, in retaliation for this act of treachery, a number of the inhabitants were executed and a portion of the city was burned. Notwithstanding the fact that, as soon as the Germans entered the city, they searched it thoroughly for concealed weapons, they claim that the townspeople were not only well supplied with rifles and ammunition, but that they even opened on them from their windows with machine-guns. Though it seems scarcely probable that the inhabitants of Louvain would attempt so mad an enterprise as to attack an overwhelming force of Germans--particularly with the terrible lesson of Aerschot still fresh in their minds--I do not care to express any opinion as to the truth of the German assertions.

One of the monuments the Germans left in their wake in Belgium ; a street scene in Louvain

The Belgians tell quite a different story. They say that, as the result of a successful Belgian offensive movement to the south of Malines, the German troops retreated in something closely akin to panic, one division falling back, after nightfall, upon Louvain. In the inky blackness the garrison, mistaking the approaching troops for Belgians, opened a deadly fire upon them. When the

130

mistake was discovered the Germans, partly in order to cover up their disastrous blunder and partly to vent their rage and chagrin, turned upon the townspeople in a paroxysm of fury. A scene of indescribable terror ensued, the soldiers, who had broken into the wine-shops and drunk themselves into a state of frenzy, practically running amuck, breaking in doors and shooting at every one they saw. That some of the citizens snatched up such weapons as came to hand and defended their homes and their women no one attempts to deny-- but this scattered and pitifully ineffectual resistance gave the Germans the very excuse they were seeking. The citizens had attacked them and they would teach the citizens, both of Louvain and of other cities which they might enter, a lasting lesson. They did. No Belgian will ever forget--or forgive-- that lesson. The orgy of blood and lust and destruction lasted for two days. Several American correspondents, among them Mr. Richard Harding Davis, who were being taken by train from Brussels to Germany, and who were held for some hours in the station at Louvain during the first night's massacre, have vividly described the horrors which they witnessed from their car window. On the second day, Mr. Hugh S. Gibson, secretary of the American Legation in Brussels, accompanied by the Swedish and Mexican charges, drove over to Louvain in a taxi-cab. Mr. Gibson told me that the Germans had dragged chairs and a dining-table from a nearby house into the middle of the square in front of the station and that some officers, already considerably the worse for drink, insisted that the three diplomatists join them in a bottle of wine. And this while the city was burning and rifles were cracking, and the dead bodies of men and women lay sprawled in the streets! From the windows of plundered and fire-blackened houses in both Aerschot and Louvain and along the road between, hung white flags made from sheets and tablecloths and pillow- cases--pathetic appeals for the mercy which was not granted.

If Belgium wishes to keep alive in the minds of her people the recollection of German military barbarism, if she desires to inculcate the coming generations with the horrors and miseries of war, if she would perpetuate the memories of the innocent townspeople who were slaughtered because they were Belgians, then she can effectually do it by preserving the ruins of Aerschot and Louvain, just as the ruins of Pompeii are preserved. Fence in these desolated cities; leave the shattered doors and the broken furniture as they are; let the bullet marks and the bloodstains remain, and it will do more than all the sermons that can be preached, than all the pictures that can be painted, than all the books that can be written, to drive home a realization of what is meant by that dreadful thing called War.

The distance from Louvain to Brussels is in the neighbourhood of twenty miles, and our car with its fluttering flags sped between lines of cheering people all the way. Men stood by the roadside with uncovered heads as they saw the Stars and Stripes whirl by; women waved their handkerchiefs while tears coursed down their cheeks. As we neared Brussels news of our coming spread, and soon we were passing between solid walls of Belgians who waved hats and canes and handkerchiefs and screamed, "Vive l'Amerique! Vive l'Amerique!" I am not ashamed to say that a lump came in my throat and tears dimmed my eyes. To these helpless, homeless, hopeless people, the red-white-and-blue banner that streamed from our windshield really was a flag of the free.

Brussels we found as quiet and orderly as London on a Sunday morning. So far as streets scenes went we might have been in Berlin. German officers and soldiers were scattered everywhere, lounging at the little iron tables in front of the cafes, or dining in the restaurants or strolling along the tree-shaded boulevards as unconcernedly as though they were in the Fatherland. Many of the officers had brought high, red-wheeled dogcarts with them, and were pleasure-driving in the outskirts of the city; others, accompanied by women who may or may not have been their wives, were picnicking in the Bois. Brussels had become, to all outward appearances at least, a German city. German flags flaunted defiantly from the roofs of the public buildings, several of which, including the Hotel de Ville, the Palais de Justice and the Cathedral, were reported to have been mined. In the whole of the great city not a single Belgian flag was to be seen. The Belgian police were still performing their routine duties under German direction. The royal palace had been converted into a hospital for German wounded. The Ministry of Foreign Affairs was occupied by the German General Staff. The walls and hoardings were plastered with proclamations signed by the military governor warning the inhabitants of the penalties which they would incur should they molest the German troops. The great square in front of the Gare du Nord, which was being used as a barracks, was guarded by a line of sentries, and no one but Germans in uniform were permitted to cross it. One other person did cross it, however, German regulations and sentries notwithstanding. Whedbee and I were lunching on Sunday noon in the front of the Palace Hotel, when a big limousine flying the American flag drew up on the other side of the square and Mr. Julius Van Hee, the American Vice-Consul at Ghent, jumped out. He caught sight of us at the same moment that we saw him and started across the square toward us. He had not gone a dozen paces before a sentry levelled his rifle and gruffly commanded him to halt.

"Go back!" shouted the sentry. "To walk across the square forbidden is."

"Go to the devil!" shouted back Van Hee. "And stop pointing that gun at me, or I'll come over and knock that spiked helmet of yours off. I'm American, and I've more right here than you have."

This latter argument being obviously unanswerable, the befuddled sentry saw nothing for it but to let him pass.

Van Hee had come to Brussels, he told us, for the purpose of obtaining some vaccine, as the supply in Ghent was running short, and the authorities were fearful of an epidemic. He also brought with him a package of letters from the German officers, many of them of distinguished families, who had been captured by the Belgians and were imprisoned at Bruges. When Van Hee had obtained his vaccine, he called on General von Ludewitz and requested a safe conduct back to Ghent.

"I'm sorry, Mr. Van Hee," said the general, who had married an American and spoke English like a New

Yorker, "but there's nothing doing. We can't permit anyone to leave Brussels at present. Perhaps in a few days------"

"A few days won't do, General," Van Hee interrupted, "I must go back to-day, at once."

"I regret to say that for the time being it is quite impossible," said the general firmly.

"I have here," said Van Hee, displaying the packet, "a large number of letters from the German officers who are imprisoned in Belgium. If I don't get the pass you don't get these letters."

"You hold a winning hand, Mr. Van Hee," said the general, laughing, as he reached for pen and paper.

But when Whedbee and I were ready to return to Antwerp it was a different matter. The German authorities, though scrupulously polite, were adamantine in their refusal to permit us to pass through the German lines. And we held no cards, as did Van Hee, with which to play diplomatic poker. So we were compelled to bluff. Telling the German commander that we would call on him again, we climbed into the car and quietly left the city by the same route we had followed upon entering it the preceding day. All along the road we found soldiers smoking the cigarettes we had distributed to them. Instead of stopping us and demanding to see our papers they waved their hands cheerily and called, "Auf wiedersehn!" As we knew that we could not get through Louvain without being stopped, we drove boldly up to headquarters and asked the general commanding the division if he would detail a staff officer to accompany us to the outer lines. (There seemed no need of mentioning the fact that we had no passes.) The general said, with profuse apologies, that he had no officer available at the moment, but hoped that a sergeant would do. We carried the sergeant with us as far as Aerschot, distributing along the way what remained of our cigarettes. At Aerschot we were detained for nearly an hour, as the officer who had visited Atlantic City, Niagara Falls and Coney Island insisted on our waiting while he sent for another officer who, until the outbreak of the war, had lived in Chicago. We tried not to show our impatience at the delay, but our hair stood on end every time a telephone bell tinkled. We were afraid that the staff in Brussels, learning of our unauthorized departure, would telephone to the outposts to stop us. It was with a heartfelt sigh of relief that we finally shook hands with our hosts and left ruined Aerschot behind us. I opened up the throttle, and the big car fled down the long, straight road which led to the Belgian lines like a hunted cat on the top of a backyard fence.

GENERAL VON BOEHN   MR. POWELL

The words " Güte Leute " (Good people) were scrawled
on the door of this house in Louvain—

—but there were no words on the door of *this* house

V. With The Spiked Helmets

It was really a Pittsburg chauffeur who was primarily responsible for my being invited to dine with the commander of the Ninth German Army. The chauffeur's name was William Van Calck and his employer was a gentleman who had amassed several millions manufacturing hats in the Smoky City. When war was declared the hat-manufacturer and his family were motoring in Austria, with Van Calck at the wheel of the car. The car being a large and powerful one, it was promptly commandeered by the Austrian military authorities; the hat-manufacturer and his family, thus dumped unceremoniously by the roadside, made their way as best they could to England; and Van Calck, who was a Belgian by birth, though a naturalized American, enlisted in the Belgian army and was detailed to drive one of the armoured motor-cars which so effectively harassed the enemy during the early part of the campaign in Flanders. Now if Van Calck hadn't come tearing into Ghent in his wheeled fortress on a sunny September morning he wouldn't have come upon a motor-car containing two German soldiers who had lost their way; if he had not met them, the two Germans would not have been wounded in the dramatic encounter which ensued; if the Germans had not been wounded it would not have been necessary for Mr. Julius Van Hee, the

American Vice- Consul, to pay a hurried visit to General von Boehn, the German commander, to explain that the people of Ghent were not responsible for the affair and to beg that no retaliatory measures be taken against the city; if Mr. Van Hee had not visited General von Boehn the question of the attitude of the American Press would not have come up for discussion; and if it had not been discussed, General von Boehn would not have sent me an invitation through Mr. Van Hee to dine with him at his headquarters and hear the German side of the question.

But perhaps I had better begin at the beginning. On September 8, then, the great German army which was moving from Brussels on France was within a few miles of Ghent. In the hope of inducing the Germans not to enter the city, whose large and turbulent working population would, it was feared, cause trouble in case of a military occupation, the burgomaster went out to confer with the German commander. An agreement was finally arrived at whereby the Germans consented to march around Ghent if certain requirements were complied with. These were that no Belgian troops should occupy the city, that the Garde Civique should be disarmed and their weapons surrendered, and that the municipality should supply the German forces with specified quantities of provisions and other supplies--the chief item, by the way, being a hundred thousand cigars.

The burgomaster had not been back an hour when a military motor- car containing two armed German soldiers appeared in the city streets. It transpired afterwards that they had been sent out to purchase medical supplies and, losing their way, had entered Ghent by mistake. At almost the same moment that the German car entered the city from the south a Belgian armoured motor-car, armed with a machine-gun and with a crew of three men and driven by the former Pittsburg chauffeur, entered from the east on a scouting expedition. The two cars, both travelling at high speed, encountered each other at the head of the Rue de l'Agneau, directly in front of the American Consulate. Vice-Consul Van Hee, standing in the doorway, was an eyewitness of what followed.

The Germans, taken completely by surprise at the sight of the grim war-car in its coat of elephant-grey bearing down upon them, threw on their power and attempted to escape, the man sitting beside the driver opening an ineffectual fire with his carbine. Regardless of the fact that the sidewalks were crowded with spectators, the Belgians opened on the fleeing Germans with their machine-gun, which spurted lead as a garden-hose spurts water. Van Calck, fearing that the Germans might escape, swerved his powerful car against the German machine precisely as a polo-player "rides off" his opponent, the machine-gun never ceasing its angry snarl. An instant later the driver of the German car dropped forward over his steering-wheel with blood gushing from a bullet-wound in the head, while his companion, also badly wounded, threw up both hands in token of surrender.

Mr. Powell, while on his way to visit General von Boehn, comes upon a party of American refugees stranded in Sattoghem. (Note the German soldier, rescued from the mob in Ghent, in the car)

Vice-Consul Van Hee instantly recognized the extremely grave consequences which might result to Ghent from this encounter, which had taken place within an hour after the burgomaster had assured the German commander that there were no Belgian soldiers in the city. Now Mr. Julius Van Hee is what is popularly known in the United States as "a live wire." He is a shirt-sleeve diplomatist who, if he thought the occasion warranted it, would not hesitate to conduct diplomatic negotiations in his night-shirt. Appreciating that as a result of this attack on German soldiers, which the Germans would probably characterize as treachery, Ghent stood in imminent danger of meeting the terrible fate of its sister-cities of Aerschot and Louvain, which were sacked and burned on no greater provocation, Mr. Van Hee jumped into his car and sought the burgomaster, whom he urged to accompany him without an instant's delay to German headquarters. The burgomaster, who had visions of being sent to Germany as a hostage, at first demurred; but Van Hee, disregarding his protestations, handed him his hat, hustled him into the car, and ordered the chauffeur to drive as though the Uhlans were behind him.

They found General von Boehn and his staff quartered in a chateau a few miles outside the city. At first the German commander was furious with anger and threatened Ghent with the same punishment he had meted out to other cities where Germans had been fired on. Van Hee took a very firm stand, however. He reminded the general that Americans have a great sentimental interest in Ghent because of the treaty of peace between England and the United States which was signed there a century ago, and he warned him that the burning of the city would do more than anything else to lose the Germans the sympathy of the American people.

"If you will give me your personal word," said the general finally, "that there will be no further attacks upon Germans who may enter the city, and that the wounded soldiers will be taken under American protection and sent to Brussels by the American Consular authorities when they have recovered, I will agree to spare Ghent and will not even demand a money indemnity."

Mr. Powell as the guest of General von Boehn and the staff of the Ninth German Army

In the course of the informal conversation which followed, General von Boehn remarked that copies of American papers containing articles by E. Alexander Powell, criticizing the Germans' treatment of the Belgian civil population, had come to his attention, and he regretted that he could not have an opportunity to talk with their author and give him the German version of the incidents in question. Mr. Van Hee said that, by a curious coincidence, I had arrived in Ghent that very morning, whereupon the general asked him to bring me out to dinner on the following day and issued a safe conduct through the German lines for the purpose.

We started early the next morning. As there was some doubt about the propriety of my taking a Belgian military driver into the German lines I drove the car myself. And, though nothing was said about a photographer, I took with me Donald Thompson. Before we passed the city limits of Ghent things began to happen. Entering a street which leads through a district inhabited by the working classes, we suddenly found our way barred by a mob of several thousand excited Flemings.

Above a sea of threatening arms and brandished sticks and angry faces rose the figures of two German soldiers, with carbines slung across their backs, mounted on work-horses which they had evidently hastily unharnessed from a wagon. Like their unfortunate comrades of the motor-car episode, they too had strayed into the city by mistake. As we approached the crowd made a concerted rush for them. A blast from my siren opened a lane for us, however, and I drove the car alongside the terrified Germans.

"Quick!" shouted Van Hee in German. "Off your horses and into the car! Hide your rifles! Take off your helmets! Sit on the floor and keep out of sight!"

The mob, seeing its prey escaping, surged about us with a roar. For a moment things looked very ugly. Van Hee jumped on the seat.

"I am the American Consul!" he shouted. "These men are under my protection! You are civilians, attacking German soldiers in uniform. If they are harmed your city will be burned about your ears."

At that moment a burly Belgian shouldered his way through the crowd and, leaping on the running-board, levelled a revolver at the Germans cowering in the tonneau. Quick as thought Thompson knocked up the man's hand, and at the same instant I threw on the power. The big car leaped forward and the mob scattered before it. It was a close call for every one concerned, but a much closer call for Ghent; for had those German soldiers been murdered by civilians in the city streets no power on earth could have saved the city from German vengeance. General von Boehn told me so himself.

A few minutes later, as playlets follow each other in quick succession on a stage, the scene changed from near tragedy to screaming farce. As we came thundering into the little town of Sotteghem, which is the Sleepy Hollow of Belgium, we saw, rising from the middle of the town square, a pyramid, at least ten feet high, of wardrobe-trunks, steamer-trunks, bags, and suit-cases. From the summit of this extraordinary monument floated a huge American flag. As our car came to a halt there rose a chorus of exclamations in all the dialects between Maine and California, and from the door of a near-by cafe came pouring a flood of Americans. They proved to be a lost detachment of that great army of tourists which, at the beginning of hostilities, started on its mad retreat for the coast, leaving Europe strewn with their belongings. This particular detachment had been cut off in Brussels by the tide of German invasion, and, as food-supplies were running short, they determined to make a dash--perhaps crawl would be a better word--for Ostend, making the journey in two lumbering farm wagons. On reaching Sotteghem, however, the Belgian drivers, hearing that the Germans were approaching, refused to go further and unceremoniously dumped their passengers in the town square. When we arrived they had been there for a day and a night and had begun to think that it was to be their future home. It was what might be termed a mixed assemblage, including several women of wealth and fashion who had been motoring on the Continent and had had their cars taken from them, two prim schoolteachers from Brooklyn, a mine-owner from West

Virginia, a Pennsylvania Quaker, and a quartet of professional tango-dancers--artists, they called themselves--who had been doing a "turn" at a Brussels music-hall when the war suddenly ended their engagement. Van Hee and I skirmished about and, after much argument, succeeded in hiring two farm-carts to transport the fugitives to Ghent. For the thirty-mile journey the thrifty peasants modestly demanded four hundred francs--and got it. When I last saw my compatriots they were perched on top of their luggage piled high on two creaking carts, rumbling down the road to Ghent with their huge flag flying above them. They were singing at the top of their voices, "We'll Never Go There Any More."

Half a mile or so out of Sotteghem our road debouched into the great highway which leads through Lille to Paris, and we suddenly found ourselves in the midst of the German army. It was a sight never to be forgotten. Far as the eye could see stretched solid columns of marching men, pressing westward, ever westward. The army was advancing in three mighty columns along three parallel roads, the dense masses of moving men in their elusive grey-green uniforms looking for all the world like three monstrous serpents crawling across the country-side.

The American flags which fluttered from our windshield proved a passport in themselves, and as we approached the close-locked ranks parted to let us pass, and then closed in behind us. For five solid hours, travelling always at express-train speed, we motored between walls of marching men. In time the constant shuffle of boots and the rhythmic swing of grey-clad arms and shoulders grew maddening, and I became obsessed with the fear that I would send the car ploughing into the human hedge on either side. It seemed that the interminable ranks would never end, and so far as we were concerned they never did end, for we never saw the head of that mighty column. We passed regiment after regiment, brigade after brigade of infantry; then hussars, cuirassiers, Uhlans, field batteries, more infantry, more field-guns, ambulances with staring red crosses painted on their canvas tops, then gigantic siege-guns, their grim muzzles pointing skyward, each drawn by thirty straining horses; engineers, sappers and miners with picks and spades, pontoon- wagons, carts piled high with what looked like masses of yellow silk but which proved to be balloons, bicyclists with carbines slung upon their backs hunter-fashion, aeroplane outfits, bearded and spectacled doctors of the medical corps, armoured motor-cars with curved steel rails above them as a protection against the wires which the Belgians were in the habit of stringing across the roads, battery after battery of pom-poms (as the quick-firers are descriptively called), and after them more batteries of spidery-looking, lean-barrelled machine-guns, more Uhlans--the sunlight gleaming on their lance-tips and the breeze fluttering their pennons into a black-and-white cloud above them, and then infantry in spiked and linen-covered helmets, more infantry and still more infantry-- all sweeping by, irresistibly as a mighty river, with their faces turned towards France.

This was the Ninth Field Army, composed of the very flower of the German Empire, including the magnificent troops of the Imperial Guard. It was first and last a fighting army. The men were all young, and they struck me as being as keen as razors and as hard as nails. Their equipment was the acme to all appearances ordinary two-wheeled farm-carts, contained "nests" of nine machine-guns which could instantly be brought into action. The medical corps was magnificent; as businesslike, as completely equipped, and as efficient as a great city hospital--as, indeed, it should be, for no hospital ever built was called upon to treat so many emergency cases. One section of the medical corps consisted wholly of pedicurists, who examined and treated the feet of the men. If a German soldier has even a suspicion of a corn or a bunion or a chafed heel and does not instantly report to the regimental pedicurist for treatment he is subject to severe punishment. He is not permitted to neglect his feet--or for that matter his teeth, or any other portion of his body--because his feet do not belong to him but to the Kaiser, and the Kaiser expects those feet kept in condition to perform long and arduous marches and to fight his battles.

The German Army pouring across the Belgian frontier into France

At one cross-roads I saw a soldier with a horse-clipping machine. An officer stood beside him and closely scanned the heads of the passing men. Whenever he spied a soldier whose hair was a fraction of an inch too long, that soldier was called out of the ranks, the clipper was run over his head as quickly and dexterously as an expert shearer fleeces sheep, and then the man, his hair once more too short to harbour dirt, ran to rejoin his company. They must have cut the hair of a hundred men an hour. It was a fascinating performance. Men on bicycles, with coils of insulated wire slung on reels between them, strung field-telephones from tree to tree, so that the general commanding could converse with any part of the fifty-mile-long column. The whole army never slept. When half was resting the other half was advancing. The German soldier is treated as a valuable machine, which must be speeded up to the highest possible efficiency. Therefore he is well fed, well shod, well clothed-- and worked as a negro teamster works a mule. Only men who are well cared-for can march thirty-five miles a day, week in and week out. Only once did I see a man ill-treated. A sentry on duty in front of the general headquarters failed to salute an officer with sufficient promptness, whereupon the officer lashed him again and again across the face with a riding-whip. Though welts rose at every blow, the soldier stood rigidly at attention and never quivered. It was not a pleasant thing to witness. Had it been a British or an American soldier who was thus treated there would have been an officer's funeral the next day.

The Ninth German Army crossing the Franco-Belgian frontier

As we were passing a German outpost a sentry ran into the road and signalled us to stop.

"Are you Americans?" he asked.

"We are," said I.

"Then I have orders to take you to the commandant," said he.

"But I am on my way to dine with General von Boehn. I have a pass signed by the General himself and I am late already."

"No matter," the man insisted stubbornly. "You must come with me. The commander has so ordered it."

So there was nothing for it but to accompany the soldier. Though we tried to laugh away our nervousness, I am quite willing to admit that we had visions of court-martials and prison cells and firing parties. You never know just where you are at with the Germans. You see, they have no sense of humour.

We found the commandant and his staff quartered at a farmhouse a half-mile down the road. He was a stout, florid-faced, boisterous captain of pioneers.

"I'm sorry to detain you," he said apologetically, "but I ordered the sentries to stop the first American car that passed, and yours happened to be the unlucky one. I have a brother in America and I wish to send a letter to him to let him know that all is well with me. Would you have the goodness to post it?"

"I'll do better than that, Captain," said I. "If you will give me your brother's name and address, and if he takes the New York World, he will read in to-morrow morning's paper that I have met you."

And the next morning, just as I had promised, Mr. F. zur Nedden of Rosebank, New York, was astonished to read in the columns of his morning paper that I had left his soldier-brother comfortably quartered in a farmhouse on the outskirts of Renaix, Belgium, in excellent health but drinking more red wine than was likely to be good for him.

The German armies were preceded by clouds of cyclists who acted as the eyes and ears of the advancing force

It was now considerably past midday, and we were within a few miles of the French frontier, when I saw the guidon which signified the presence of the head of the army, planted at the entrance to a splendid old chateau. As we passed between the stately gateposts, whirled up the splendid, tree-lined drive and came to a stop in front of the terrace, a dozen officers came running out to meet us. So cordial and informal were their greetings that I felt as though I were being welcomed at a country-house in America instead of the headquarters of a German army in the field. So perfect was the field-telephone service that the staff had been able to keep in touch with our progress ever since, five hours before, we had entered the German lines, and had waited dinner for us. General von Boehn I found to be a red-faced, grey-moustached, jovial old warrior, who seemed very much worried for fear that we were not getting enough to eat, and particularly enough to drink. He explained that the Belgian owners of the chateau had had the bad taste to run away and take their servants with them, leaving only one bottle of champagne in the cellar. That bottle was good, however, as far as it went. Nearly all the officers spoke English, and during the meal the conversation was chiefly of the United States, for one of them had been attached to the German Embassy at Washington and knew the golf-course at Chevy Chase better than I do myself; another had fished in California and shot elk in Wyoming; and a third had attended the army school at Fort Riley. After dinner we grouped ourselves on the terrace and Thompson made photographs of us. They are probably the only ones--in this war, at least--of a German general and an American war correspondent who is not under arrest. Then we gathered about a table on which was spread a staff map of the war area and got down to serious business.

The general began by asserting that the accounts of atrocities perpetrated by German troops on Belgian non-combatants were lies.

"Look at these officers about you," he said. "They are gentlemen, like yourself. Look at the soldiers marching past in the road out there. Most of them are the fathers of families. Surely you do not believe that they would do the unspeakable things they have been accused of?"

"Three days ago, General," said I, "I was in Aerschot. The whole town is now but a ghastly, blackened ruin."

"When we entered Aerschot," was the reply, "the son of the burgomaster came into the room where our officers were dining and assassinated the Chief of Staff. What followed was retribution. The townspeople got only what they deserved."

"But why wreak your vengeance on women and children?" I asked.

"None have been killed," the general asserted positively.

"I'm sorry to contradict you, General," I asserted with equal positiveness, "but I have myself seen their bodies. So has Mr. Gibson, the secretary of the American Legation in Brussels, who was present during the destruction of Louvain."

"Of course," replied General von Boehn, "there is always danger of women and children being killed during street fighting if they insist on coming into the streets. It is unfortunate, but it is war."

"But how about a woman's body I saw with the hands and feet cut off? How about the white-haired man and his son whom I helped to bury outside of Sempst, who had been killed merely because a retreating Belgian soldier had shot a German soldier outside their house? There were twenty-two bayonet wounds in the old man's face. I counted them. How about the little girl, two years old, who was shot while in her mother's arms by a Uhlan and whose funeral I attended at Heyst-op-den-Berg? How about the old man near Vilvorde who was hung by his hands from the rafters of his house and roasted to death by a bonfire being built under him?"

The general seemed taken aback by the exactness of my information.

"Such things are horrible if true," he said. "Of course, our soldiers, like soldiers in all armies, sometimes get out of hand and do things which we would never tolerate if we knew it. At Louvain, for example, I sentenced two soldiers to twelve years' penal servitude each for assaulting a woman."

"Apropos of Louvain," I remarked, "why did you destroy the library?"

"We regretted that as much as anyone else," was the answer. "It caught fire from burning houses and we could not save it."

"But why did you burn Louvain at all?" I asked.

"Because the townspeople fired on our troops. We actually found machine-guns in some of the houses. And," smashing his fist down upon the table, "whenever civilians fire upon our troops we will teach them a lasting lesson. If women and children insist on getting in the way of bullets, so much the worse for the women and children."

"How do you explain the bombardment of Antwerp by Zeppelins?" I inquired.

"Zeppelins have orders to drop their bombs only on fortifications and soldiers," he answered.

"As a matter of fact," I remarked, "they destroyed only private houses and innocent civilians, several of whom were women. If one of those bombs had dropped two hundred yards nearer my hotel I wouldn't be here to-day smoking one of your excellent cigars."

"That is a calamity which, thank God, didn't happen," he replied.

"If you feel for my safety as deeply as that, General," I said, earnestly, "you can make quite sure of my coming to no harm by sending no more Zeppelins."

"Well, Herr Powell," he said, laughing, "we will think about it. And," he continued gravely, "I trust that you will tell the American people, through your great paper, what I have told you to-day. Let them hear our side of this atrocity business. It is only justice that they should be made familiar with both sides of the question."

Artillery of the Imperial Guard near Renaix, Belgium

I have quoted my conversation with General von Boehn as nearly verbatim as I can remember it. I have no comments to make. I will leave it to my readers to decide for themselves just how convincing were the answers of the German General Staff--for General von Boehn was but its mouthpiece--to the Belgian accusations. Before we began our conversation I asked the general if my photographer, Thompson, might be permitted to take photographs of the great army which was passing. Five minutes later Thompson whirled away in a military motor-car, ciceroned by the officer who had attended the army school at Fort Riley. It seems that they stopped the car beside the road, in a place where the light was good, and when Thompson saw approaching a regiment or a battery or a squadron of which he wished a picture he would tell the officer, whereupon the officer would blow a whistle and the whole column would halt.

"Just wait a few minutes until the dust settles," Thompson would remark, lighting a cigar, and the Ninth Imperial Army, whose columns stretched over the country-side as far as the eye could see, would stand in its tracks until the air was sufficiently clear to get a good picture.

A field battery of the Imperial Guard rumbled past and Thompson made some remark about the accuracy of the American gunners at Vera Cruz.

"Let us show you what our gunners can do," said the officer, and he gave an order. There were more orders--a perfect volley of them. A bugle shrilled, eight horses strained against their collars, the drivers cracked their whips, the cannoneers put their shoulders to the wheels, and a gun left the road and swung into position in an adjacent field. On a knoll three miles away an ancient windmill was beating the air with its huge wings. A shell hit the windmill and tore it into splinters.

"Good work," Thompson observed critically. "If those fellows of yours keep on they'll be able to get a job in the American navy when the war is over."

In all the annals of modern war I do not believe that there is a parallel to this little Kansas photographer halting, with peremptory hand, an advancing army and leisurely photographing it, regiment by regiment, and then having a field-gun of the Imperial Guard go into action solely to gratify his curiosity.

They were very courteous and hospitable to me, those German officers, and I was immensely interested with all that I saw. But, when all is said and done, they impressed me not as human beings, who have weaknesses and virtues, likes and dislikes of their own, but rather as parts, more or less important, of a mighty and highly efficient machine which is directed and controlled by a cold and calculating intelligence in far-away Berlin. That machine has about as much of the human element as a meat-chopper, as a steam- roller, as the death-chair at Sing Sing. Its mission is to crush, obliterate, destroy, and no considerations of civilization or chivalry or humanity will affect it. I think that the Germans, with their grim, set faces, their monotonous uniforms, and the ceaseless shuffle, shuffle, shuffle of their boots must have gotten on my nerves, for it was with a distinct feeling of relief that I turned the bonnet of my car once more towards Antwerp and my friends the Belgians.

The defence of Termonde. Belgian infantry firing from trenches built with head-covers as a protection from shrapnel

VI. On The Belgian Battle-Line

In writing of the battles in Belgium I find myself at a loss as to what names to give them. After the treaty-makers have affixed their signatures to a piece of parchment and the arm-chair historians have settled down to the task of writing a connected account of the campaign, the various engagements will doubtless be properly classified and labelled--and under the names which they will receive in the histories we, who were present at them, will probably not recognize them at all. Until such time, then, as history has granted them the justice of perspective, I can only refer to them as "the fight at Sempst" or "the first engagement at Alost" or "the battle of Vilvorde" or "the taking of Termonde." Not only this, but the engagements that seemed to us to be battles, or remarkably lifelike imitations of battles, may be dismissed by the historians as unimportant skirmishes and contacts, while those engagements that we carelessly referred to at the time as "scraps" may well prove, in the light of future events, to have been of far greater significance than we realized. I don't even know how many engagements I witnessed, for I did not take the trouble to keep count. Thompson, who was with me from the beginning of the campaign to the end, told a reporter who interviewed him upon his return to London that we had been present at thirty-two engagements, large and small. Though I do not vouch, mind you, for the accuracy of this assertion, it is not as improbable as it sounds, for, from the middle of August to the fall of Antwerp in the early part of October, it was a poor day that didn't produce a fight of some sort. The fighting in Belgium at this stage of the war may be said to have been confined to an area within a triangle whose corners were Antwerp, Aerschot and Termonde. The southern side of this triangle, which ran somewhat to the south of Malines, was nearly forty miles in length, and it was this forty-mile front, extending from Aerschot on the east to Termonde on the west, which, during the earlier stages of the campaign, formed the Belgian battle-line. As the campaign progressed and the Germans developed their offensive, the Belgians were slowly forced back within the converging sides of the triangle until they were squeezed into the angle formed by Antwerp, where they made their last stand.

What the Germans did to Termonde. Before setting fire to the town they systematically sprayed the houses with petrol

The Mother Superior in front of the ruins of her convent in Termonde, which was sacked and burned by the Germans

The theatre of operations was, from the standpoint of a professional onlooker like myself, very inconsiderately arranged. Nature had provided neither orchestra-stalls nor boxes. All the seats were bad. In fact it was quite impossible to obtain a good view of the stage and of the uniformed actors who were presenting the most stupendous spectacle in all history upon it. The whole region, you see, was absolutely flat--as flat as the top of a table--and there wasn't anything even remotely resembling a hill anywhere. To make matters worse, the country was criss-crossed by a perfect network of rivers and brooks and canals and ditches; the highways and the railways, which had to be raised to keep them from being washed out by the periodic inundations, were so thickly screened by trees as to be quite useless for purposes of observation; and in the rare places where a rise in the ground might have enabled one to get a comprehensive view of the surrounding country, dense groves of trees or red-and-white villages almost invariably intervened. One could be within a few hundred yards of the firing-line and literally not see a thing save the fleecy puffs of bursting shrapnel. Indeed, I don't know what we should have done had it not been for the church towers. These were conveniently sprinkled over the landscape-- every cluster of houses seemed to have one--and did their best to make up for the region's topographical shortcomings. The only disadvantage attaching to the use of the church-spires as places to view the fighting from was that the military observers and the officers controlling the fire of the batteries used them for the same purpose. The enemy knew this, of course, and almost the first thing he did, therefore, was to open fire on them with his artillery and drive those observers out. This accounts for the fact that in many sections of Belgium there is not a church-spire left standing. When we ascended a church tower, therefore, for the purpose of obtaining a general view of an engagement, we took our chances and we knew it. More than once, when the enemy got the range and their shells began to shriek and yowl past the belfry in which I was stationed, I have raced down the rickety ladders at a speed which, under normal conditions, would probably have resulted in my breaking my neck. In view of the restrictions imposed upon correspondents in the French and Russian theatres of war, I suppose that instead of finding fault with the seating arrangements I should thank my lucky stars that I did not have to write my dispatches with the aid of an ordnance-map and a guide-book in a hotel bedroom a score or more of miles from the firing-line.

The Belgians who drove the Germans out of Termonde

The Belgian field army consisted of six divisions and a brigade of cavalry and numbered, on paper at least, about 180,000 men. I very much doubt, however, if King Albert had in the field at anyone time more than 120,000 men--a very large proportion of whom were, of course, raw recruits. Now the Belgian army, when all is said and done, was not an army according to the Continental definition; it was not much more than a glorified police force, a militia. No one had ever dreamed that it would be called upon to fight, and hence, when war came, it was wholly unprepared. That it was able to offer the stubborn and heroic resistance which it did to the advance of the German legions speaks volumes for Belgian stamina and courage. Many of the troops were armed with rifles of an obsolete pattern, the supply of ammunition was insufficient, and though the artillery was on the whole of excellent quality, it was placed at a tremendous disadvantage by the superior range and calibre of the German field- guns. The men did not even have the protection afforded by neutral- coloured uniforms, but fought from first to last in clothes of blue and green and blazing scarlet. As I stood one day in the Place de Meir in Antwerp and watched a regiment of mud-bespattered guides clatter past, it was hard to believe that I was living in the twentieth century and not in the beginning of the nineteenth, for instead of serviceable uniforms of grey or drab or khaki, these men wore the befrogged green jackets, the cherry-coloured breeches, and the huge fur busbies which characterized the soldiers of Napoleon.

The carabineers, for example, wore uniforms of bottle-green and queer sugar-loaf hats of patent leather which resembled the headgear of the Directoire period. Both the grenadiers and the infantry of the line marched and fought and slept in uniforms of heavy blue cloth piped with scarlet and small, round, visorless fatigue-caps which afforded no protection from either sun or rain. Some of the men remedied this by fitting their caps with green reading-shades, such as undergraduates wear when they are cramming for examinations, so that at first glance a regiment looked as though its ranks were filled with either jockeys or students. The gendarmes--who, by the way, were always to be found where the fighting was hottest--were the most unsuitably uniformed of all, for the blue coats and silver aiguillettes and towering bearskins which served to impress the simple country-folk made splendid targets for the German marksmen. This medley of picturesque and brilliant uniforms was wonderfully effective, of course, and whenever I came upon a group of lancers in sky-blue and yellow lounging about the door of a wayside tavern or met a patrol of guides in their green jackets and scarlet breeches trotting along a country-road, I always had the feeling that I was looking at a painting by Meissonier or Detaille.

Belgian artillery officer watching effect of battery fire from observation
ladder

At the beginning of the war the Belgian cavalry was
as well mounted as that of any European army, many of
the officers having Irish hunters, while the men were
mounted on Hungarian-bred stock. The almost incessant
campaigning, combined with lack of proper food and
care, had its effect upon the horses, however, and before
the campaign in Flanders was half over the cavalry

mounts were a raw- boned and sorry-looking lot. The Belgian field artillery was horsed magnificently: the sturdy, hardy animals native to Luxembourg and the Ardennes making admirable material for gun-teams, while the great Belgian draught-horses could scarcely have been improved upon for the army's heavier work.

Speaking of cavalry, the thing that I most wanted to see when I went to the war was a cavalry charge. I had seen mounted troops in action, of course, both in Africa and in Asia, but they had brown skins and wore fantastic uniforms. What I wanted to see was one of those charges such as Meissonier used to paint--scarlet breeches and steel helmets and a sea of brandished sword-blades and all that sort of thing. But when I confided my wish to an American army officer whom I met on the boat going over he promptly discouraged me. "Cavalry charges are a thing of the past," he asserted. "There will never be one again. The modern high-power rifle has made them impossible. Henceforward cavalry will only be used for scouting purposes or as mounted infantry." He spoke with great positiveness, I remember, having been, you see, in both the Cuban and Philippine campaigns. According to the textbooks and the military experts and the armchair tacticians he was perfectly right; I believe that all of the writers on military subjects agree in saying that cavalry charges are obsolete as a form of attack. But the trouble with the Belgians was that they didn't play the war-game according to the rules in the book. They were very primitive in their conceptions of warfare. Their idea was that whenever they got within sight of a German regiment to go after that regiment and exterminate it, and they didn't care whether in doing it they used horse, foot, or guns. It was owing, therefore, to this total disregard for the rules laid down in the textbooks that I saw my cavalry charge. Let me tell you about it while I have the chance, for there is no doubt that cavalry charges are getting scarce and I may never see another.

German soldier being buried on the battlefield near Alost

It was in the region between Termonde and Alost. This is a better country for cavalry to manoeuvre in than most parts of Flanders, for sometimes one can go almost a mile without being stopped by a canal. A considerable force of Germans had pushed north from Alost and the Belgian commander ordered a brigade of cavalry, composed of the two regiments of guides and, if I remember rightly, two regiments of lancers, to go out and drive them back. After a morning spent in skirmishing and manoeuvring for position, the Belgian cavalry commander got his Germans where he wanted them. The Germans were in front of a wood, and between them and the Belgians lay as pretty a stretch of open country as a cavalryman could ask for. Now the Germans occupied a strong position, mind you, and the proper thing to have done according to the books would have been to have demoralized them with shell-fire and then to have followed it up with an infantry attack. But the grizzled old Belgian commander did nothing of the sort. He had fifteen hundred troopers who were simply praying for a chance to go at the Germans with cold steel, and he gave them the chance they wanted. Tossing away his cigarette and tightening the chin-strap of his busby, he trotted out in front of his men. "Right into line!" he bellowed. Two long lines--one the guides, in green and scarlet, the other the lancers, in blue and yellow--spread themselves across the fields. "Trot!" The bugles squealed the order. "Gallop!" The forest of lances dropped from vertical to horizontal and the cloud of gaily fluttering pennons changed into a bristling hedge of steel. "Charge!" came the order, and the spurs went home. "Vive la Belgique! Vive la Belgique!" roared the troopers--and the Germans, not liking the look of those long and cruel lances, fell back precipitately into the wood where the troopers could not follow them. Then, their work having been accomplished, the cavalry came trotting back again. Of course, from a military standpoint it was an affair of small importance, but so far as colour and action and excitement were concerned it was worth having gone to Belgium to see.

After the German occupation of Brussels, the first engagement of sufficient magnitude to be termed a battle took place on August 25 and 26 in the Sempst-Elewyt-Eppeghem-Vilvorde region, midway between Brussels and Malines. The Belgians had in action four divisions, totalling about sixty thousand men, opposed to which was a considerably heavier force of Germans. To get a clear conception of the battle one must picture a fifty-foot-high railway embankment, its steeply sloping sides heavily wooded, stretching its length across a fertile, smiling country-side like a monstrous green snake. On this line, in time of peace, the bloc trains made the journey from Antwerp to Brussels in less than an hour. Malines, with its historic buildings and its famous cathedral, lies on one side of this line and the village of Vilvorde on the other, five miles separating them. On the 25th the Belgians, believing the Brussels garrison to have been seriously weakened and the German communications poorly guarded, moved out in force from the shelter of the Antwerp forts and assumed a vigorous offensive. It was like a terrier attacking a bulldog.

Five thousand women waiting for bread in the courtyard of the Hôtel de Ville at Malines. A month before there was no such thing as pauperism or want in Belgium

They drove the Germans from Malines by the very impetus of their attack, but the Germans brought up heavy reinforcements, and by the morning of the 26th the Belgians were in a most perilous position. The battle hinged on the possession of the railway embankment had gradually extended, each army trying to outflank the other, until it was being fought along a front of twenty miles. At dawn on the second day an artillery duel began across the embankment, the German fire being corrected by observers in captive balloons. By noon the Germans had gotten the range and a rain of shrapnel was bursting about the Belgian batteries, which limbered up and retired at a trot in perfect order. After the guns were out of range I could see the dark blue masses of the supporting Belgian infantry slowly falling back, cool as a winter's morning. Through an oversight, however, two battalions of carabineers did not receive the order to retire and were in imminent danger of being cut off and destroyed.

Then occurred one of the bravest acts that I have ever seen. To reach them a messenger would have to traverse a mile of open road, swept by-shrieking shrapnel and raked by rifle-fire. There was about one chance in a thousand of a man getting to the end of that road alive. A colonel standing beside me under a railway-culvert summoned a gendarme, gave him the necessary orders, and added, "Bonne chance, mon brave." The man, a fierce-moustached fellow who would have gladdened the heart of Napoleon, knew that he was being sent into the jaws of death, but he merely saluted, set spurs to his horse, and tore down the road, an archaic figure in his towering bearskin. He reached the troops uninjured and gave the order for them to retreat, but as they fell back the German gunners got the range and with marvellous accuracy dropped shell after shell into the running column. Soon road and fields were dotted with corpses in Belgian blue.

Time after time the Germans attempted to carry the railway embankment with the bayonet, but the Belgians met them with blasts of lead which shrivelled the grey columns as leaves are shrivelled by an autumn wind. By mid-afternoon the Belgians and Germans were in places barely a hundred yards apart, and the rattle of musketry sounded like a boy drawing a stick along the palings of a picket-fence. During the height of the battle a Zeppelin slowly circled over the field like a great vulture awaiting a feast. So heavy was the fighting that the embankment of a branch railway from which I viewed the afternoon's battle was literally carpeted with the corpses of Germans who had been killed during the morning. One of them had died clasping a woman's picture. He was buried with it still clenched in his hand. I saw peasants throw twelve bodies into one grave. One peasant would grasp a corpse by the shoulders and another would take its feet and they would give it a swing as though it were a sack of meal. As I watched these inanimate forms being carelessly tossed into the trench it was hard to make myself believe that only a few hours before they had been sons or husbands or fathers and that somewhere across the Rhine women and children were waiting and watching and praying for them. At a hamlet near Sempst I helped to bury an aged farmer and his son, inoffensive peasants, who had been executed by the Germans because a retreating Belgian soldier had shot a Uhlan in front of their farmhouse. Not content with shooting them, they had disfigured them almost beyond recognition. There were twenty-two bayonet wounds in the old man's face. I know, for I counted them.

By four o'clock all the Belgian troops were withdrawn except a thin screen to cover the retreat. As I wished to see the German advance I remained on the railway embankment on the outskirts of Sempst after all the Belgians, save a picket of ten men, had been withdrawn from the village. I had my car waiting in the road below with the motor running. As the German infantry would have to advance across a mile of open fields it was obvious that I would have ample time in which to get away. The Germans prefaced their advance by a terrific cannonade. The air was filled with whining shrapnel. Farmhouses collapsed amid puffs of brown smoke. The sky was smeared in a dozen places with the smoke of burning hamlets. Suddenly a soldier crouching beside me cried, "Les Allemands! Les Allemands!" and from the woods which screened the railway-embankment burst a long line of grey figures, hoarsely cheering. At almost the same moment I heard a sudden splutter of shots in the village street behind me and my driver screamed, "Hurry for your life, monsieur! The Uhlans are upon us!" In my desire to see the main German advance it had never occurred to me that a force of the enemy's cavalry might slip around and take us in the flank, which was exactly what had happened. It was three hundred yards to the car and a freshly ploughed field lay between, but I am confident that I broke the world's record for the distance. As I leaped into the car and we shot down the road at fifty miles an hour, the Uhlans cantered into the village, the sunlight striking on their lance- tips. It was a close call.

The retreat from Malines provided a spectacle which I shall never forget. For twenty miles every road was jammed with clattering cavalry, plodding infantry, and rumbling batteries, the guns, limbers, and caissons still covered with the green boughs which had been used to mask their position from German aeroplanes. Gendarmes in giant bearskins, chasseurs in uniforms of green and yellow, carabineers with their shiny leather hats, grenadiers, infantry of the line, guides, lancers, sappers and miners with picks and spades, engineers with pontoon-wagons, machine-guns drawn by dogs, ambulances with huge Red Cross flags fluttering above them, and cars, cars, cars, all the dear old familiar American makes among them, contributed to form a mighty river flowing towards Antwerp. Malines formerly had a population of fifty thousand people, and forty-five thousand of these fled when they heard that the Germans were returning. The scenes along the road were heart-rending in their pathos. The very young and the very old, the rich and the well- to-do and the poverty-stricken, the lame and the sick and the blind, with the few belongings they had been able to save in sheet-wrapped bundles on their backs or piled in push-carts, clogged the roads and impeded the soldiery. These people were abandoning all that they held most dear to pillage and destruction. They were completely terrorized by the Germans. But the Belgian army was not terrorized. It was a retreating army but it was victorious in retreat. The soldiers were cool, confident, courageous, and gave me the feeling that if the German giant left himself unguarded a single instant little Belgium would drive home a solar-plexus blow.

For many days after its evacuation by the Belgians, Malines occupied an unhappy position midway between the contending armies, being alternately bombarded by the Belgians and the Germans. The latter, instead of endeavouring to avoid damaging the splendid cathedral, whose tower, three hundred and twenty-five feet high, is the most conspicuous landmark in the region, seemed to take a grim pleasure in directing their fire upon the ancient building. The great clock, the largest in Belgium, was destroyed; the famous stained-glass windows were broken; the exquisite carvings were shattered; and shells, crashing through the walls and roof, converted the beautiful interior into a heap of debris. As there were no Belgian troops in Malines at this time, and as this fact was perfectly well known to the Germans, this bombardment of an undefended city and the destruction of its historic monuments struck me as being peculiarly wanton and not induced by any military necessity. It was, of course, part and parcel of the German policy of terrorism and intimidation. The bombardment of cities, the destruction of historic monuments, the burning of villages, and, in many cases, the massacre of civilians was the price which the Belgians were forced to pay for resisting the invader.

In order to ascertain just what damage had been done to the city, and particularly to the cathedral, I ran into Malines in my car during a pause in the bombardment. As the streets were too narrow to permit of turning the car around, and as it was more than probable that we should have to get out in a hurry, Roos suggested that we run in backward, which we did, I standing up in the tonneau, field-glasses glued to my eyes, on the look-out for lurking Germans. I don't recall ever having had a more eerie experience than that surreptitious visit to Malines. The city was as silent and deserted as a cemetery; there was not a human being to be seen; and as we cautiously advanced through the narrow, winding streets, the vacant houses echoed the throbbing of the motor with a racket which was positively startling. Just as we reached the square in front of the cathedral a German shell came shrieking over the house-tops and burst with a shattering crash in the upper story of a building a few yards away. The whole front of that building came crashing down about us in a cascade of brick and plaster. We did not stay on the order of our going. No. We went out of that town faster than any automobile every went out of it before. We went so fast, in fact, that we struck and killed the only remaining inhabitant. He was a large yellow dog.

Owing to strategic reasons the magnitude and significance of the great four days' battle which was fought in mid-September between the Belgian field army and the combined German forces in Northern Belgium was carefully masked in all official communications at the time, and, in the rush of later events, its importance was lost sight of. Yet the great flanking movement of the Allies in France largely owed its success to this determined offensive movement on the part of the Belgians, who, as it afterwards proved, were acting in close co-operation with the French General Staff. This unexpected sally, which took the Germans completely by surprise, not only compelled them to concentrate all their available forces in Belgium, but, what was far more important, it necessitated the hasty recall of their Third and Ninth armies, which were close to the French frontier and whose addition to the German battle-line in France might well have turned the scales in Germany's favour. In addition the Germans had to bring up their Landwehr and Landsturm regiments from the south of Brussels, and a naval division composed of fifteen thousand sailors and marines was also engaged. It is no exaggeration, then, to say that the success of the Allies on the Aisne was in great measure due to the sacrifices made on this occasion by the Belgian army. Every available man which the Germans could put into the field was used to hold a line running through Sempst, Weerde, Campenhout, Wespelaer, Rotselaer, and Holsbeek. The Belgians lay to the north-east of this line, their left resting on Aerschot and their centre at Meerbeek. Between the opposing armies stretched the Malines-Louvain canal, along almost the entire length of which fighting as bloody as any in the war took place.

Before the assault on Weerde. Belgian infantry lying on the ground to avoid rifle and shell fire

To describe this battle--I do not even know by what name it will be known to future generations--would be to usurp the duties of the historian, and I shall only attempt, therefore, to tell you of that portion of it which I saw with my own eyes. On the morning of September 13 four Belgian divisions moved southward from Malines, their objective being the town of Weerde, on the Antwerp- Brussels railway. It was known that the Germans occupied Weerde in force, so throughout the day the Belgian artillery, masked by heavy woods, pounded away incessantly. By noon the enemy's guns ceased to reply, which was assumed by the jubilant Belgians to be a sign that the German artillery had been silenced. At noon the Belgian First Division moved forward and Thompson and I, leaving the car in front of a convent over which the Red Cross flag was flying, moved forward with it. Standing quite by itself in the middle of a field, perhaps a mile beyond the convent, was a two-story brick farmhouse. A hundred yards in front of the farmhouse stretched the raised, stone-paved, tree-lined highway which runs from Brussels to Antwerp, and on the other side of the highway was Weerde. Sheltering ourselves as much as possible in the trenches which zigzagged across the field, and dashing at full speed across the open places which were swept by rifle-fire, we succeeded in reaching the farmhouse. Ascending to the garret, we broke a hole through the tiled roof and found ourselves looking down upon the battle precisely as one looks down on a cricket match from the upper tier of seats at Lord's. Lying in the deep ditch which bordered our side of the highway was a Belgian infantry brigade, composed of two regiments of carabineers and two regiments of chasseurs a pied, the men all crouching in the ditch or lying prone upon the ground. Five hundred yards away, on the other side of the highway, we could see through the trees the whitewashed walls and red pottery roofs of Weerde, while a short distance to the right, in a heavily wooded park, was a large stone chateau. The only sign that the town was occupied was a pall of blue-grey vapour which hung over it and a continuous crackle of musketry coming from it, though occasionally, through my glasses, I could catch glimpses of the lean muzzles of machine-guns protruding from the upper windows of the chateau.

Now you must bear in mind the fact that in this war soldiers fired from the trenches for days on end without once getting a glimpse of the enemy. They knew that somewhere opposite them, in that bit of wood, perhaps, or behind that group of buildings, or on the other side of that railway-embankment, the enemy was trying to kill them just as earnestly as they were trying to kill him. But they rarely got a clear view of him save in street fighting and, of course, when he was advancing across open country. Soldiers no longer select their man and pick him off as one would pick off a stag, because the great range of modern rifles has put the firing-lines too far apart for that sort of thing. Instead, therefore, of aiming at individuals, soldiers aim at the places where they believe those individuals to be. Each company commander shows his men their target, tells them at what distance to set their sights, and controls their expenditure of ammunition, the fire of infantry generally being more effective when delivered in bursts by sections.

What I have said in general about infantry being unable to see the target at which they are firing was particularly true at Weerde owing to the dense foliage which served to screen the enemy's position. Occasionally, after the explosion of a particularly well-placed Belgian shell, Thompson and I, from our hole in the roof and with the aid of our high-power glasses, could catch fleeting glimpses of scurrying grey-clad figures, but that was all. The men below us in the trenches could see nothing except the hedges, gardens, and red-roofed houses of a country town. They knew the enemy was there, however, from the incessant rattle of musketry and machine-guns and from the screams and exclamations of those of their fellows who happened to get in the bullets' way.

Late in the afternoon word was passed down the line that the German guns had been put out of action, that the enemy was retiring and that at 5.30 sharp the whole Belgian line would advance and take the town with the bayonet. Under cover of artillery fire so continuous that it sounded like thunder in the mountains, the Belgian infantry climbed out of the trenches and, throwing aside their knapsacks, formed up behind the road preparatory to the grand assault. A moment later a dozen dog batteries came trotting up and took position on the left of the infantry. At 5.30 to the minute the whistles of the officers sounded shrilly and the mile-long line of men swept forward cheering. They crossed the roadway, they scrambled over ditches, they climbed fences, they pushed through hedges, until they were within a hundred yards of the line of buildings which formed the outskirts of the town. Then hell itself broke loose. The whole German front, which for several hours past had replied but feebly to the Belgian fire, spat a continuous stream of lead and flame. The rolling crash of musketry and the ripping snarl of machine-guns were stabbed by the vicious pom-pom-pom- pom-pom of the quick-firers. From every window of the three-storied chateau opposite us the lean muzzles of mitrailleuses poured out their hail of death. I have seen fighting on four continents, but I have never witnessed so deadly a fire as that which wiped out the head of the Belgian column as a sponge wipes out figures on a slate.

The Germans had prepared a trap and the Belgians had walked--or rather charged--directly into it. Three minutes later the dog batteries came tearing back on a dead run. That should have been a signal that it was high time for us to go, but, in spite of the fact that a storm was brewing, we waited to see the last inning. Then things began to happen with a rapidity that was bewildering. Back through the hedges, across the ditches, over the roadway came the Belgian infantry, crouching, stooping, running for their lives, Every now and then a soldier would stumble, as though he had stubbed his toe, and throw out his arms and fall headlong. A bullet had hit him. The road was sprinkled with silent forms in blue and green. The fields were sprinkled with them too. One man was hit as he was struggling to get through a hedge and died standing, held upright by the thorny branches. Men with blood streaming down their faces, men with horrid crimson patches on their tunics, limped, crawled, staggered past, leaving scarlet trails behind them. A young officer of chasseurs, who had been recklessly exposing himself while trying to check the retreat of his men, suddenly spun around on his heels, like one of those wooden toys which the curb vendors sell, and then crumpled up, as though all the bone and muscle had gone out of him. A man plunged into a half-filled ditch and lay there, with his head under water. I could see the water slowly redden.

Bullets began to smash the tiles above us. "This is no place for two innocent little American boys," remarked Thompson, shouldering his camera. I agreed with him. By the time we reached the ground the Belgian infantry was half a mile in our rear, and to reach the car we had to cross nearly a mile of open field. Bullets were singing across it and kicking up little spurts of brown earth where they struck. We had not gone a hundred yards when the German artillery, which the Belgians so confidently asserted had been silenced, opened with shrapnel. Have you ever heard a winter gale howling and shrieking through the tree-tops? Of course. Then you know what shrapnel sounds like, only it is louder. You have no idea though how extremely annoying shrapnel is, when it bursts in your immediate vicinity. You feel as though you would like nothing in the world so much as to be suddenly transformed into a woodchuck and have a convenient hole. I remembered that an artillery officer had told me that a burst of shrapnel from a battery two miles away will spread itself over an eight-acre field, and every time I heard the moan of an approaching shell I wondered if it would decide to explode in the particular eight-acre field in which I happened to be.

As though the German shell-storm was not making things sufficiently uncomfortable for us, when we were half-way across the field two Belgian soldiers suddenly rose from a trench and covered us with their rifles. "Halt! Hands up!" they shouted. There was nothing for it but to obey them. We advanced with our hands in the air but with our heads twisted upward on the look-out for shrapnel. As we approached they recognized us. "Oh, you're the Americans," said one of them, lowering his rifle. "We couldn't see your faces and we took you for Germans. You'd better come with us. It's getting too hot to stay here." The four of us started on a run for a little cluster of houses a few hundred yards away. By this time the shells were coming across at the rate of twenty a minute.

"Suppose we go into a cellar until the storm blows over," suggested Roos, who had joined us. "I'm all for that," said I, making a dive for the nearest doorway. "Keep away from that house!" shouted a Belgian soldier who suddenly appeared from around a corner. "The man who owns it has gone insane from fright. He's upstairs with a rifle and he's shooting at every one who passes." "Well, I call that damned inhospitable," said Thompson, and Roos and I heartily agreed with him. There was nothing else for it, therefore, but to make a dash for the car. We had left it standing in front of a convent over which a Red Cross flag was flying on the assumption that there it would be perfectly safe. But we found that we were mistaken. The Red Cross flag did not spell protection by any means. As we came within sight of the car a shell burst within thirty feet of it, a fragment of the projectile burying itself in the door. I never knew of a car taking so long to crank. Though it was really probably only a matter of seconds before the engine started it seemed to us, standing in that shell-swept road, like hours.

Darkness had now fallen. A torrential rain had set in. The car slid from one side of the road to the other like a Scotchman coming home from celebrating Bobbie Burns's birthday and repeatedly threatened to capsize in the ditch. The mud was ankle-deep and the road back to Malines was now in the possession of the Germans, so we were compelled to make a detour through a deserted country- side, running through the inky blackness without lights so as not to invite a visit from a shell. It was long after midnight when, cold, wet and famished, we called the password to the sentry at the gateway through the barbed-wire entanglements which encircled Antwerp and he let us in. It was a very lively day for every one concerned and there were a few minutes when I thought that I would never see the Statue of Liberty again.

VII. The Coming Of The British

Imagine, if you please, a professional heavy-weight prize-fighter, with an abnormally long reach, holding an amateur bantam-weight boxer at arm's length with one hand and hitting him when and where he pleased with the other. The fact that the little man was not in the least afraid of his burly antagonist and that he got in a vicious kick or jab whenever he saw an opening would not, of course, have any effect on the outcome of the unequal contest. Now that is almost precisely what happened when the Germans besieged Antwerp, the enormously superior range and calibre of their siege-guns enabling them to pound the city's defences to pieces at their leisure without the defenders being able to offer any effective resistance.

Though Antwerp was to all intents and purposes a besieged city for many weeks prior to its capture, it was not until the beginning of the last week in September that the Germans seriously set to work of destroying its fortifications. When they did begin, however, their great siege pieces pounded the forts as steadily and remorselessly as a trip-hammer pounds a bar of iron. At the time the Belgian General Staff believed that the Germans were using the same giant howitzers which demolished the forts at Liege, but in this they were mistaken, for, as it transpired later, the Antwerp fortifications owed their destruction to Austrian guns served by Austrian artillerymen. Now guns of this size can only be fired from specially prepared concrete beds, and these beds, as we afterwards learned, had been built during the preceding month behind the embankment of the railway which runs from Malines to Louvain, thus accounting for the tenacity with which the Germans had held this railway despite repeated attempts to dislodge them. At this stage of the investment the Germans were firing at a range of upwards of eight miles, while the Belgians had no artillery that was effective at more than six. Add to this the fact that the German fire was remarkably accurate, being controlled and constantly corrected by observers stationed in balloons, and that the German shells were loaded with an explosive having greater destructive properties than either cordite or shimose powder, and it will be seen how hopeless was the Belgian position.

The scenes along the Lierre-St. Catherine-Waelhem sector, against which the Germans at first focussed their attack, were impressive and awesome beyond description. Against a livid sky rose pillars of smoke from burning villages. The air was filled with shrieking shell and bursting shrapnel. The deep-mouthed roar of the guns in the forts and the angry bark of the Belgian field-batteries were answered at intervals by the shattering crash of the German high-explosive shells. When one of these big shells--the soldiers dubbed them "Antwerp expresses"--struck in a field it sent up a geyser of earth two hundred feet in height. When they dropped in a river or canal, as sometimes happened, there was a waterspout. And when they dropped in a village, that village disappeared from the map.

While we were watching the bombardment from a rise in the Waelhem road a shell burst in the hamlet of Waerloos, whose red- brick houses were clustered almost at our feet. A few minutes later a procession of fugitive villagers came plodding up the cobble- paved highway. It was headed by an ashen-faced peasant pushing a wheelbarrow with a weeping woman clinging to his arm. In the wheelbarrow, atop a pile of hastily collected household goods, was sprawled the body of a little boy. He could not have been more than seven. His little knickerbockered legs and play-worn shoes protruded grotesquely from beneath a heap of bedding. When they lifted it we could see where the shell had hit him. Beside the dead boy sat his sister, a tot of three, with blood trickling from a flesh- wound in her face. She was still clinging convulsively to a toy lamb which had once been white but whose fleece was now splotched with red. Some one passed round a hat and we awkwardly tried to express our sympathy through the medium of silver. After a little pause they started on again, the father stolidly pushing the wheelbarrow, with its pathetic load, before him. It was the only home that family had.

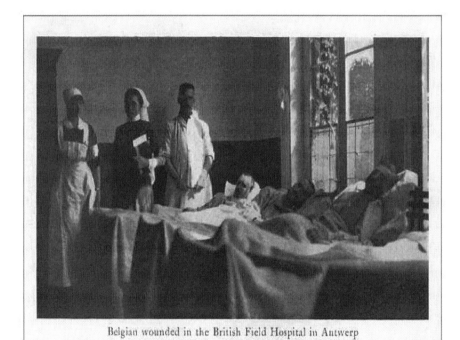

Belgian wounded in the British Field Hospital in Antwerp

One of the bravest acts that I have ever seen was performed by an American woman during the bombardment of Waelhem. Her name was Mrs. Winterbottom; she was originally from Boston, and had married an English army officer. When he went to the front in France she went to the front in Belgium, bringing over her car, which she drove herself, and placing it at the disposal of the British Field Hospital. After the fort of Waelhem had been silenced and such of the garrison as were able to move had been withdrawn, word was received at ambulance headquarters that a number of dangerously wounded had been left behind and that they would die unless they received immediate attention. To reach the fort it was necessary to traverse nearly two miles of road swept by shell-fire. Before anyone realized what was happening a big grey car shot down the road with the slender figure of Mrs. Winterbottom at the wheel. Clinging to the running-board was her English chauffeur and beside her sat my little Kansas photographer, Donald Thompson. Though the air was filled with the fleecy white patches which look like cotton-wool but are really bursting shrapnel, Thompson told me afterwards that Mrs. Winterbottom was as cool as though she were driving down her native Commonwealth Avenue on a Sunday morning. When they reached the fort shells were falling all about them, but they filled the car with wounded men and Mrs. Winterbottom started back with her blood-soaked freight for the Belgian lines.

Thompson remained in the fort to take pictures. When darkness fell he made his way back to the village of Waelhem, where he found a regiment of Belgian infantry. In one of the soldiers Thompson recognized a man who, before the war, had been a waiter in the St. Regis Hotel in New York and who had been detailed to act as his guide and interpreter during the fighting before Termonde. This man took Thompson into a wine-shop where a detachment of soldiers was quartered, gave him food, and spread straw upon the floor for him to sleep on. Shortly after midnight a forty-two centimetre shell struck the building. Of the soldiers who were sleeping in the same room as Thompson nine were killed and fifteen more who were sleeping upstairs, the ex-waiter among them. Thompson told me that when the ceiling gave way and the mangled corpses came tumbling down upon him, he ran up the street with his hands above his head, screaming like a madman. He met an officer whom he knew and they ran down the street together, hoping to get out of the doomed town. Just then a projectile from one of the German siege- guns tore down the long, straight street, a few yards above their heads. The blast of air which it created was so terrific that it threw them down. Thompson said that it was like standing close to the edge of the platform at a wayside station when the Empire State Express goes by. When his nerve came back to him he pulled a couple of cigars out of his pocket and offered one to the officer. Their hands trembled so, he said afterwards, that they used up half a box of matches before they could get their cigars lighted.

Belgian infantry going into action at Lierre under heavy fire

I am inclined to think that the most bizarre incident I saw during the bombardment of the outer forts was the flight of the women inmates of a madhouse at Duffel.

There were three hundred women in the institution, many of them violently insane, and the nuns in charge, assisted by soldiers, had to take them across a mile of open country, under a rain of shells, to a waiting train. I shall not soon forget the picture of that straggling procession winding its slow way across the stubble-covered fields. Every few seconds a shell would burst above it or in front of it or behind it with a deafening explosion. Yet, despite the frantic efforts of the nuns and soldiers, the women would not be hurried. When a shell burst some of them would scream and cower or start to run, but more of them would stop in their tracks and gibber and laugh and clap their hands like excited children. Then the soldiers would curse under their breath and push them roughly forward and the nuns would plead with them in their soft, low voices, to hurry, hurry, hurry. We, who were watching the scene, thought that few of them would reach the train alive, yet not one was killed or wounded. The Arabs are right: the mad are under God's protection.

One of the most inspiring features of the campaign in Belgium was the heroism displayed by the priests and the members of the religious orders. Village cures in their black cassocks and shovel hats, and monks in sandals and brown woollen robes, were everywhere. I saw them in the trenches exhorting the soldiers to fight to the last for

God and the King; I saw them going out on to the battlefield with stretchers to gather the wounded under a fire which made veterans seek shelter; I saw them in the villages where the big shells were falling, helping to carry away the ill and the aged; I saw them in the hospitals taking farewell messages and administering the last sacrament to the dying; I even saw them, rifle in hand, on the firing-line, fighting for the existence of the nation. To these soldiers of the Lord I raise my hat in respect and admiration. The people of Belgium owe them a debt that they can never repay.

In the days before the war it was commonly said that the Church was losing ground in Belgium; that religion was gradually being ousted by socialism. If this were so, I saw no sign of it in the nation's days of trial. Time and time again I saw soldiers before going into battle drop on their knees and cross themselves and murmur a hasty prayer. Even the throngs of terrified fugitives, flying from their burning villages, would pause in their flight to kneel before the little shrines along the wayside. I am convinced, indeed, that the ruthless destruction of religious edifices by the Germans and the brutality which they displayed toward priests and members of the religious orders was more responsible than any one thing for the desperate resistance which they met with from the Belgian peasantry.

Belgian masked battery in action during the defence of the Néthe. Notice how cleverly the guns are concealed from observers in aeroplanes

By the afternoon of October 3 things were looking very black for Antwerp. The forts composing the Lierre-Waelhem sector of the outer line of defences had been pounded into silence by the German siege-guns; a strong German force, pushing through the breach thus made, had succeeded in crossing the Nethe in the face of desperate opposition; the Belgian troops, after a fortnight of continuous fighting, were at the point of exhaustion;

the hospitals were swamped by the streams of wounded which for days past had been pouring in; over the city hung a cloud of despondency and gloom, for the people, though kept in complete ignorance of the true state of affairs, seemed oppressed with a sense of impending disaster.

Ward in a Belgian hospital struck by a German shell

When I returned that evening to the Hotel St. Antoine from the battle-front, which was then barely half a dozen miles outside the city, the manager stopped me as I was entering the lift.

"Are you leaving with the others, Mr. Powell?" he whispered.

"Leaving for where? With what others?" I asked sharply.

"Hadn't you heard?" he answered in some confusion. "The members of the Government and the Diplomatic Corps are leaving for Ostend by special steamer at seven in the morning. It has just been decided at a Cabinet meeting. But don't mention it to a soul. No one is to know it until they are safely gone."

I remember that as I continued to my room the corridors smelled of smoke, and upon inquiring its cause I learned that the British Minister, Sir Francis Villiers, and his secretaries were burning papers in the rooms occupied by the British Legation. The Russian Minister, who was superintending the packing of his trunks in the hall, stopped me to say good-bye. Imagine my surprise, then, upon going down to breakfast the following morning, to meet Count Goblet d'Alviella, the Vice-

President of the Senate and a minister of State, leaving the dining-room.

"Why, Count!" I exclaimed, "I had supposed that you were well on your way to Ostend by this time."

"We had expected to be," explained the venerable statesman, "but at four o'clock this morning the British Minister sent us word that Mr. Winston Churchill had started for Antwerp and asking us to wait and hear what he has to say."

At one o'clock that afternoon a big drab-coloured touring-car filled with British naval officers tore up the Place de Meir, its horn sounding a hoarse warning, took the turn into the narrow Marche aux Souliers on two wheels, and drew up in front of the hotel. Before the car had fairly come to a stop the door of the tonneau was thrown violently open and out jumped a smooth-faced, sandy-haired, stoop- shouldered, youthful-looking man in the undress Trinity House uniform. There was no mistaking who it was. It was the Right Hon. Winston Churchill. As he darted into the crowded lobby, which, as usual at the luncheon-hour, was filled with Belgian, French, and British staff officers, diplomatists, Cabinet Ministers and correspondents, he flung his arms out in a nervous, characteristic gesture, as though pushing his way through a crowd. It was a most spectacular entrance and reminded me for all the world of a scene in a melodrama where the hero dashes up, bare-headed, on a foam-flecked horse, and saves the heroine or the old homestead or the family fortune, as the case may be.

While lunching with Sir Francis Villiers and the staff of the British Legation, two English correspondents approached and asked Mr. Churchill for an interview.

"I will not talk to you," he almost shouted, bringing his fist down upon the table. "You have no business to be in Belgium at this time. Get out of the country at once."

It happened that my table was so close that I could not help but overhear the request and the response, and I remember remarking to the friends who were dining with me: "Had Mr. Churchill said that to me, I should have answered him, 'I have as much business in Belgium at this time, sir, as you had in Cuba during the Spanish-American War.'"

An hour later I was standing in the lobby talking to M. de Vos, the Burgomaster of Antwerp, M. Louis Franck, the Antwerp member of the Chamber of Deputies, American Consul-General Diederich and Vice-Consul General Sherman, when Mr. Churchill rushed past us on his way to his room. He impressed one as being always in a tearing hurry. The Burgomaster stopped him, introduced himself, and expressed his anxiety regarding the fate of the city. Before he had finished Churchill was part-way up the stairs.

"I think everything will be all right now, Mr. Burgomaster," he called down in a voice which could be distinctly heard throughout the lobby. "You needn't worry. We're going to save the city."

Whereupon most of the civilians present heaved sighs of relief. They felt that a real sailor had taken the wheel. Those of us who were conversant with the situation were also relieved because we took it for granted that Mr. Churchill would not have made so confident and public an assertion unless ample reinforcements in men and guns were on the way. Even then the words of this energetic, impetuous young man did not entirely reassure me, for from the windows of my room I could hear the German guns quite plainly. They had come appreciably nearer.

That afternoon and the three days following Mr. Churchill spent in inspecting the Belgian position. He repeatedly exposed himself upon the firing-line and on one occasion, near Waelhem, had a rather narrow escape from a burst of shrapnel. For some unexplainable reason the British censorship cast a veil of profound secrecy over Mr. Churchill's visit to Antwerp. The story of his arrival, just as I have related it above, I telegraphed that same night to the New York World, yet it never got through, nor did any of the other dispatches which I sent during his four days' visit. In fact, it was not until after Antwerp had fallen that the British public was permitted to learn that the Sea Lord had been in Belgium.

Had it not been for the promises of reinforcements given to the King and the Cabinet by Mr. Churchill, there is no doubt that the Government would have departed for Ostend when originally planned and that the inhabitants of Antwerp, thus warned of the extreme gravity of the situation, would have had ample time to leave the city with a semblance of comfort and order, for the railways leading to Ghent and to the Dutch frontier were still in operation and the highways were then not blocked by a retreating army.

The first of the promised reinforcements arrived on Sunday evening by special train from Ostend. They consisted of a brigade of the Royal Marines, perhaps two thousand men in all, well drilled and well armed, and several heavy guns. They were rushed to the southern front and immediately sent into the trenches to relieve the worn-out Belgians. On Monday and Tuesday the balance of the British expeditionary force, consisting of between five and six thousand men of the Volunteer Naval Reserve, arrived from the coast, their ammunition and supplies being brought by road, via Bruges and Ghent, in London motor-buses. When this procession of lumbering vehicles, placarded with advertisements of teas, tobaccos, whiskies, and current theatrical attractions and bearing the signs "Bank," "Holborn," "Piccadilly," "Shepherd's Bush," "Strand," rumbled through the streets of Antwerp, the populace went mad. "The British had come at last! The city was saved! Vive les Anglais! Vive Tommy Atkins!"

Blocking the road at Meux Diene, from which the British and Belgians were compelled to retreat

I witnessed the detrainment of the naval brigades at Vieux Dieu and accompanied them to the trenches north of Lierre. As they tramped down the tree-bordered, cobble-paved high road, we heard, for the first time in Belgium, the lilting refrain of that music-hall ballad which had become the English soldiers' marching song:

It's a long way to Tipperary, It's a long way to go; It's a long way to Tipperary To the sweetest girl I know!

Good-bye, Piccadilly! Farewell, Leicester Square! It's a long, long way to Tipperary; But my heart's right there!

Many and many a one of the light-hearted lads with whom I marched down the Lierre road on that October afternoon were destined never again to feel beneath their feet the flags of Piccadilly, never again to lounge in Leicester Square.

They were as clean-limbed, pleasant-faced, wholesome-looking a lot of young Englishmen as you would find anywhere, but to anyone who had had military experience it was evident that, despite the fact that they were vigorous and courageous and determined to do their best, they were not "first-class fighting men." To win in war, as in the prize-ring, something more than vigour and courage and determination are required; to those qualities must be added experience and training, and experience and training were precisely what those naval reservists lacked. Moreover, their equipment left much to be desired. For example, only a very small proportion had pouches to carry the regulation one hundred and fifty rounds. They were, in fact, equipped very much as many of the American militia organizations were equipped when suddenly called out for strike duty in the days before the reorganization of the National Guard. Even the officers--those, at least, with whom I talked--seemed to be as deficient in field experience as the men. Yet these raw troops were rushed into trenches which were in most cases unprotected by head-covers, and, though unsupported by effective artillery, they held those trenches for three days under as murderous a shell-fire as I have ever seen and then fell back in perfect order. What the losses of the Naval Division were I do not know. In Antwerp it was generally understood that very close to a fifth of the entire force was killed or wounded--upwards of three hundred cases were, I was told, treated in one hospital alone--and the British Government officially announced that sixteen hundred were forced across the frontier and interned in Holland.

No small part in the defence of the city was played by the much- talked-about armoured train, which was built under the supervision of Lieutenant-Commander Littlejohn in the yards of the Antwerp Engineering Company at Hoboken. The train consisted of four large coal-trucks with sides of armour-plate sufficiently high to afford protection to the crews of the 4.7 naval guns--six of which were brought from England for the purpose, though there was only time to mount four of them--and between each gun-truck was a heavily- armoured goods-van for ammunition, the whole being drawn by a small locomotive, also steel-protected. The guns were served by Belgian artillerymen commanded by British gunners and each gun- truck carried, in addition, a detachment of infantry in the event of the enemy getting to close quarters. Personally, I am inclined to believe that the chief value of this novel contrivance lay in the moral encouragement it lent to the defence, for its guns, though more powerful, certainly, than anything that the Belgians possessed, were wholly outclassed, both in range and calibre, by the German artillery. The German officers whom I questioned on the subject after the occupation told me that the fire of the armoured train caused them no serious concern and did comparatively little damage.

By Tuesday night a boy scout could have seen that the position of Antwerp was hopeless. The Austrian siege guns had smashed and silenced the chain of supposedly impregnable forts to the south of the city with the same businesslike dispatch with which the same type of guns had smashed and silenced those other supposedly impregnable forts at Liege and Namur. Through the opening thus made a German army corps had poured to fling itself against the second line of defence, formed by the Ruppel and the Nethe. Across the Nethe, under cover of a terrific artillery fire, the Germans threw their pontoon-bridges, and when the first bridges were destroyed by the Belgian guns they built others, and when these were destroyed in turn they tried again, and at the third attempt they succeeded. With the helmeted legions once across the river, it was all over but the shouting, and no one knew it better than the Belgians, yet, heartened by the presence of the little handful of English, they fought desperately, doggedly on. Their forts pounded to pieces by guns which they could not answer, their ranks thinned by a murderous rain of shot and shell, the men heavy-footed and heavy-eyed from lack of sleep, the horses staggering from exhaustion, the ambulance service broken down, the hospitals helpless before the flood of wounded, the trenches littered with the dead and dying, they still held back the German legions.

By this time the region to the south of Antwerp had been transformed from a peaceful, smiling country-side into a land of death and desolation. It looked as though it had been swept by a great hurricane, filled with lightning which had missed nothing. The blackened walls of what had once been prosperous farm-houses, haystacks turned into heaps of smoking carbon, fields slashed across with trenches, roads rutted and broken by the great wheels of guns and transport wagons--these scenes were on every hand. In the towns and villages along the Nethe, where the fighting was heaviest, the walls of houses had fallen into the streets and piles of furniture, mattresses, agricultural machinery, and farm carts showed where the barricades and machine-guns had been. The windows of many of the houses were stuffed with mattresses and pillows, behind which the riflemen had made a stand. Lierre and Waelhem and Duffel were like sieves dripping blood. Corpses were strewn everywhere. Some of the dead were spread-eagled on their backs as though exhausted after a long march, some were twisted and crumpled in attitudes grotesque and horrible, some were propped up against the walls of houses to which they had tried to crawl in their agony.

All of them stared at nothing with awful, unseeing eyes. It was one of the scenes that I should like to forget. But I never can.

On Tuesday evening General de Guise, the military governor of Antwerp, informed the Government that the Belgian position was fast becoming untenable and, acting on this information, the capital of Belgium was transferred from Antwerp to Ostend, the members of the Government and the Diplomatic Corps leaving at daybreak on Wednesday by special steamer, while at the same time Mr. Winston Churchill departed for the coast by automobile under convoy of an armoured motorcar. His last act was to order the destruction of the condensers of the German vessels in the harbour, for which the Germans, upon occupying the city, demanded an indemnity of twenty million francs.

As late as Wednesday morning the great majority of the inhabitants of Antwerp remained in total ignorance of the real state of affairs. Morning after morning the Matin and the Metropole had published official communiqués categorically denying that any of the forts had been silenced and asserting in the most positive terms that the enemy was being held in check all along the line. As a result of this policy of denial and deception, the people of Antwerp went to sleep on Tuesday night calmly confident that in a few days more the Germans would raise the siege from sheer discouragement and depart. Imagine what happened, then, when they awoke on Wednesday morning, October 7, to learn that the Government had stolen away between two days without issuing so much as a word of warning, and to find staring at them from every wall and hoarding proclamations signed by the military governor announcing that the bombardment of the city was imminent, urging all who were able to leave instantly, and advising those who remained to shelter themselves behind sand-bags in their cellars. It was like waiting until the entire first floor of a house was in flames and the occupants' means of escape almost cut off, before shouting "Fire!"

A seventeen-year-old Belgian girl whose father, mother, brothers, and sister had been killed

No one who witnessed the exodus of the population from Antwerp will ever forget it. No words can adequately describe it. It was not a flight; it was a stampede. The sober, slow-moving, slow-thinking Flemish townspeople were suddenly transformed into a herd of terror-stricken cattle. So complete was the

German enveloping movement that only three avenues of escape remained open: westward, through St. Nicolas and Lokeren, to Ghent; north- eastward across the frontier into Holland; down the Scheldt toward Flushing. Of the half million fugitives--for the exodus was not confined to the citizens of Antwerp but included the entire population of the country-side for twenty miles around--probably fully a quarter of a million escaped by river. Anything that could float was pressed into service: merchant steamers, dredgers, ferry-boats, scows, barges, canal-boats, tugs, fishing craft, yachts, rowing-boats, launches, even extemporized rafts. There was no attempt to enforce order. The fear-frantic people piled aboard until there was not even standing room on the vessels' decks. Of all these thousands who fled by river, but an insignificant proportion were provided with food or warm clothing or had space in which to lie down. Yet through two nights they huddled together on the open decks in the cold and the darkness while the great guns tore to pieces the city they had left behind them. As I passed up the crowded river in my launch on the morning after the first night's bombardment we seemed to be followed by a wave of sound--a great murmur of mingled anguish and misery and fatigue and hunger from the homeless thousands adrift upon the waters.

The scenes along the highways were even more appalling, for here the retreating soldiery and the fugitive civilians were mixed in inextricable confusion. By mid-afternoon on Wednesday the road from Antwerp to Ghent, a distance of forty miles, was a solid mass of refugees, and the same was true of every road, every lane, every footpath leading in a westerly or a northerly direction. The people fled in motor-cars and in carriages, in delivery-wagons, in moving- vans, in farm-carts, in omnibuses, in vehicles drawn by oxen, by donkeys, even by cows, on horseback, on bicycles, and there were thousands upon thousands afoot. I saw men trundling wheelbarrows piled high with bedding and with their children perched upon the bedding. I saw sturdy young peasants carrying their aged parents in their arms. I saw women of fashion in fur coats and high-heeled shoes staggering along clinging to the rails of the caissons or to the ends of wagons. I saw white-haired men and women grasping the harness of the gun-teams or the stirrup-leathers of the troopers, who, themselves exhausted from many days of fighting, slept in their saddles as they rode. I saw springless farm-wagons literally heaped with wounded soldiers with piteous white faces; the bottoms of the wagons leaked and left a trail of blood behind them. A very old priest, too feeble to walk, was trundled by two young priests in a handcart. A young woman, an expectant mother, was tenderly and anxiously helped on by her husband. One of the saddest features of all this dreadful procession was the soldiers, many of them wounded, and so bent with fatigue from many days of marching and fighting that they could hardly raise their feet. One infantryman who could bear his boots no longer had tied them to the cleaning-rod of his rifle. Another had strapped his boots to his cowhide knapsack and limped forward with his swollen feet in felt slippers. Here were a group of Capuchin monks abandoning their monastery; there a little party of white-faced nuns shepherding the flock of children--many of them fatherless--who had been entrusted to their care. The confusion was beyond all imagination, the clamour deafening: the rattle of wheels, the throbbing of motors, the clatter of hoofs, the cracking of whips, the curses of the drivers, the groans of the wounded, the cries of women, the whimpering of children, threats, pleadings, oaths, screams, imprecations, and always the monotonous shuffle, shuffle, shuffle of countless weary feet.

The fields and the ditches between which these processions of disaster passed were strewn with the prostrate forms of those who, from sheer exhaustion, could go no further. And there was no food for them, no shelter. Within a few hours after the exodus began the country-side was as bare of food as the Sahara is of grass.

Time after time I saw famished fugitives pause at farmhouses and offer all of their pitifully few belongings for a loaf of bread; but the kind- hearted country-people, with tears streaming down their cheeks, could only shake their heads and tell them that they had long since given all their food away. Old men and fashionably gowned women and wounded soldiers went out into the fields and pulled up turnips and devoured them raw--for there was nothing else to eat. During a single night, near a small town on the Dutch frontier, twenty women gave birth to children in the open fields. No one will ever know how many people perished during that awful flight from hunger and exposure and exhaustion; many more, certainly, than lost their lives in the bombardment.

Abandoned and starving dogs howled mournfully in front
of what had once been their homes

After the bombardment of Antwerp. Sometimes a shell
would slice the whole front of a house away, leaving the
interior exposed, like the interior on a stage

VIII. The Fall Of Antwerp

The bombardment of Antwerp began about ten o'clock on the evening of Wednesday, October 7. The first shell to fall within the city struck a house in the Berchem district, killing a fourteen-year-old boy and wounding his mother and little sister. The second decapitated a street-sweeper as he was running for shelter. Throughout the night the rain of death continued without cessation, the shells falling at the rate of four or five a minute. The streets of the city were as deserted as those of Pompeii. The few people who remained, either because they were willing to take their chances or because they had no means of getting away, were cowering in their cellars. Though the gas and electric lights were out, the sky was rosy from the reflection of the petrol-tanks which the Belgians had set on fire; now and then a shell would burst with the intensity of magnesium, and the quivering beams of two searchlights on the forts across the river still further lit up the ghastly scene. The noise was deafening. The buildings seemed to rock and sway. The very pavements trembled. Mere words are inadequate to give a conception of the horror of it all. There would come the hungry whine of a shell passing low over the house-tops, followed, an instant later, by a shattering crash, and the whole facade of the building that had been struck would topple into the street in a cascade of brick and stone and plaster. It was not until Thursday night, however, that the Germans brought their famous forty-two- centimetre guns into action. The effect of these monster cannon was appalling. So tremendous was the detonation that it sounded as though the German batteries were firing salvoes. The projectiles they were now raining upon the city weighed a ton apiece and had the destructive properties of that much nitroglycerine. We could hear them as they came. They made a roar in the air which sounded at first like an approaching express train, but which rapidly rose in volume until the atmosphere quivered with the howl of a cyclone. Then would come an explosion which jarred the city to its very foundations.

Over the shivering earth rolled great clouds of dust and smoke. When one of these terrible projectiles struck a building it did not merely tear away the upper stories or blow a gaping aperture in its walls: the whole building crumbled, disintegrated, collapsed, as though flattened by a mighty hand. When they exploded in the open street they not only tore a hole in the pavement the size of a cottage cellar, but they sliced away the facades of all the houses in the immediate vicinity, leaving their interiors exposed, like the interiors upon a stage. Compared with the "forty-twos" the shell and shrapnel fire of the first night's bombardment was insignificant and harmless. The thickest masonry was crumpled up like so much cardboard. The stoutest cellars were no protection if a shell struck above them. It seemed as though at times the whole city was coming down about our ears. Before the bombardment had been in progress a dozen hours there was scarcely a street in the southern quarter of the city-- save only the district occupied by wealthy Germans, whose houses remained untouched-- which was not obstructed by heaps of fallen masonry. The main thoroughfares were strewn with fallen electric light and trolley wires and shattered poles and branches lopped from trees. The sidewalks were carpeted with broken glass. The air was heavy with the acrid fumes of smoke and powder. Abandoned dogs howled mournfully before the doors of their deserted homes. From a dozen quarters of the city columns of smoke by day and pillars of fire by night rose against the sky.

One of the "wildcat" trains which the Belgians sent into the German lines outside Antwerp and which caused great damage

Owing to circumstances--fortunate or unfortunate, as one chooses to view them--I was not in Antwerp during the first night's bombardment. You must understand that a war correspondent, no matter how many thrilling and interesting things he may be able to witness, is valueless to the paper which employs him unless he is able to get to the end of a telegraph wire and tell the readers of that newspaper what is happening. In other words, he must not only gather the news but he must deliver it. Otherwise his usefulness ceases. When, therefore, on Wednesday morning, the telegraph service from Antwerp abruptly ended, all trains and boats stopped running, and the city was completely cut off from communication with the outside world, I left in my car for Ghent, where the telegraph was still in operation, to file my dispatches. So dense was the mass of retreating soldiery and fugitive civilians which blocked the approaches to the pontoon-bridge, that it took me four hours to get across the Scheldt, and another four hours, owing to the slow driving necessitated by the terribly congested roads, to cover the forty miles to Ghent. I had sent my dispatches, had had a hasty dinner, and was on the point of starting back to Antwerp, when Mr. Johnson, the American Consul at Ostend, called me up by telephone. He told me that the Minister of War, then at Ostend, had just sent him a package containing the keys of buildings and dwellings belonging to German residents of Antwerp who had been expelled at the beginning of the war, with the request that they be transmitted to the German commander immediately the German troops entered the city, as it was feared that, were these places found to be locked, it might lead to the doors being broken open and thus give the Germans a pretext for sacking. Mr. Johnson asked me if I would remain in Ghent until he could come through in his car with the keys and if I would assume the responsibility of seeing that the keys reached the German commander. I explained to Mr. Johnson that it was imperative that I should return to Antwerp immediately; but when he insisted that, under the circumstances, it was clearly my duty to take the keys through to Antwerp, I promised to await his arrival, although by so doing I felt that I was imperilling the interests of the newspaper which was employing me. Owing to the congested condition of the roads Mr. Johnson was unable to reach Ghent until Thursday morning.

Peasants building a bridge for Mr. Powell's motor-car across an inundated area near Doel

By this time the highroad between Ghent and Antwerp was utterly impassable--one might as well have tried to paddle a canoe up the rapids at Niagara as to drive a car against the current of that river of terrified humanity--so, taking advantage of comparatively empty by- roads, I succeeded in reaching Doel, a fishing village on the Scheldt a dozen miles below Antwerp, by noon on Thursday.

By means of alternate bribes and threats, Roos, my driver, persuaded a boatman to take us up to Antwerp in a small motor- launch over which, as a measure of precaution, I raised an American flag. As long as memory lasts there will remain with me, sharp and clear, the recollection of that journey up the Scheldt, the surface of which was literally black with vessels with their loads of silent misery. It was well into the afternoon and the second day's bombardment was at its height when we rounded the final bend in the river and the lace-like tower of the cathedral rose before us. Shells were exploding every few seconds, columns of grey-green smoke rose skyward, the air reverberated as though to a continuous peal of thunder. As we ran alongside the deserted quays a shell burst with a terrific crash in a street close by, and our boatman, panic-stricken, suddenly reversed his engine and backed into the middle of the river. Roos drew his pistol.

"Go ahead!" he commanded. "Run up to the quay so that we can land." Before the grim menace of the automatic the man sullenly obeyed.

"I've a wife and family at Doel," he muttered. "If I'm killed there'll be no one to look after them."

"I've a wife and family in America," I retorted. "You're taking no more chances than I am."

I am not in the least ashamed to admit, however, that as we ran alongside the Red Star quays--the American flag was floating above them, by the way--I would quite willingly have given everything I possessed to have been back on Broadway again. A great city which has suddenly been deserted by its population is inconceivably depressing. Add to this the fact that every few seconds a shell would burst somewhere behind the row of buildings that screened the waterfront, and that occasionally one would clear the house-tops altogether and, moaning over our heads, would drop into the river and send up a great geyser, and you will understand that Antwerp was not exactly a cheerful place in which to land. There was not a soul to be seen anywhere. Such of the inhabitants as remained had taken refuge in their cellars, and just at that time a deep cellar would have looked extremely good to me. On the other hand, as I argued with myself there was really an exceedingly small chance of a shell exploding on the particular spot where I happened to be standing, and if it did--well, it seemed more dignified, somehow, to be killed in the open than to be crushed to death in a cellar like a cornered rat.

The retreat from Antwerp. The Belgian Army passing through Lokoren

The rearguard of the Antwerp garrison

An unexploded shell that landed in the garden of the
house occupied by Donald Thompson during the
bombardment of Antwerp

About ten o'clock in the evening the bombardment slackened for a time and the inhabitants of Antwerp's underworld began to creep out of their subterranean hiding-places and slink like ghosts along the quays in search of food. The great quantities of food-stuffs and other provisions which had been taken from the captured German vessels at the beginning of the war had been stored in hastily- constructed warehouses upon the quays, and it was not long before the rabble, undeterred by the fear of the police and willing to chance the shells, had broken in the doors and were looting to their hearts' content. As a man staggered past under a load of wine bottles, tinned goods and cheeses, our boatman, who by this time had become reconciled to sticking by us, inquired wistfully if he might do a little looting too. "We've no food left down the river," he urged, "and I might just as well get some of those provisions for my family as to let the Germans take them." Upon my assenting he disappeared into the darkness of the warehouse with a hand-truck. He was not the sort who did his looting by retail, was that boatman.

By midnight Roos and I were shivering as though with ague, for the night had turned cold, we had no coats, and we had been without food since leaving Ghent that morning. "I'm going to do a little looting on my own account." I finally announced. "I'm half frozen and almost starved and I'm not going to stand around here while there's plenty to eat and drink over in that warehouse." I groped my way through the blackness to the doorway and entering, struck a match. By its flickering light I saw a case filled with bottles in straw casings. From their shape they looked to be bottles of champagne. I reached for one eagerly, but just as my fingers closed about it a shell burst overhead. At least the crash was so terrific that it seemed as though it had burst overhead, though I learned afterward that it had exploded nearly a hundred yards away. I ran for my life, clinging, however, to the bottle. "At any rate, I've found something to drink," I said to Roos exultantly, when my heart had ceased its pounding. Slipping off the straw cover I struck a match to see the result of my maiden attempt at looting. I didn't particularly care whether it was wine or brandy. Either would have tasted good. It was neither. It was a bottle of pepsin bitters!

At daybreak we started at full speed down the river for Doel, where we had left the car, as it was imperative that I should get to the end of a telegraph wire, file my dispatches, and get back to the city. They told me at Doel that the nearest telegraph office was at a little place called L'Ecluse, on the Dutch frontier, ten miles away.

We were assured that there was a good road all the way and that we could get there and back in an hour. So we could have in ordinary times, but these were extraordinary times and the Belgians, in order to make things as unpleasant as possible for the Germans, had opened the dykes and had begun to inundate the country. When we were about half-way to L'Ecluse, therefore, we found our way barred by a miniature river and no means of crossing it. It was in such circumstances that Roos was invaluable. Collecting a force of peasants, he set them to work chopping down trees and with these trees we built a bridge sufficiently strong to support the weight of the car. Thus we came into L'Ecluse.

But when the stolid Dutchman in charge of the telegraph office saw my dispatches he shrugged his shoulders discouragingly. "It is not possible to send them from here," he explained. "We have no instrument here but have to telephone everything to Hulst, eight miles away. As I do not understand English it would be impossible to telephone your dispatches." There seemed nothing for it but to walk to Hulst and back again, for the Dutch officials refused to permit me to take the car, which was a military one, across the frontier. Just at that moment a young Belgian priest--Heaven bless him!--who had overheard the discussion, approached me. "If you will permit me, monsieur," said he, "I will be glad to take your dispatches through to Hulst myself. I understand their importance. And it is well that the people in England and in America should learn what is happening here in Belgium and how bitterly we need their aid." Those dispatches were, I believe, the only ones to come out of Antwerp during the bombardment. The fact that the newspaper readers in London and New York and San Francisco were enabled to learn within a few hours of what had happened in the great city on the Scheldt was due, not to any efforts of mine, but to this little Belgian priest.

But when we got back to Doel the launch was gone. The boatman, evidently not relishing another taste of bombardment, had decamped, taking his launch with him. And neither offers of money nor threats nor pleadings could obtain me another one. For a time it looked as though getting back to Antwerp was as hopeless as getting to the moon. Just as I was on the point of giving up in despair, Roos appeared with a gold-laced official whom he introduced as the chief quarantine officer. "He is going to let you take the quarantine launch," said he. I don't know just what arguments Roos had brought to bear, and I was careful not to inquire, but ten minutes later I was sitting in lonely state on the after-deck of a trim black yacht and we were streaking it up the river at twenty miles an hour. As I knew that the fall of the city was only a matter of hours, I refused to let Roos accompany me and take the chances of being made a prisoner by the Germans, but ordered him instead to take the car, while there was yet time, and make his way to Ostend. I never saw him again. By way of precaution, in case the Germans should already be in possession of the city, I had taken the two American flags from the car and hoisted them on the launch, one from the mainmast and the other at the taffrail. It was a certain satisfaction to know that the only craft that went the wrong way of the river during the bombardment flew the Stars and Stripes. As we came within sight of the quays, the bombardment, which had become intermittent, suddenly broke out afresh and I was compelled to use both bribes and threats--the latter backed up by a revolver--to induce the crew of the launch to run in and land me at the quay. An hour after I landed the city surrendered.

When the Germans had finished with Termonde, the bells in the tower of the burned Hôtel de Ville crashed to the pavement

The withdrawal of the garrison from Antwerp began on Thursday and, everything considered, was carried out in excellent order, the troops being recalled in units from the outer line, marched through the city and across the pontoon-bridge which spans the Scheldt and thence down the road to St. Nicolas to join the retreating field army. What was implied in the actual withdrawal from contact with the enemy will be appreciated when I explain the conditions which existed. In places the lines were not two hundred yards apart and for the defenders no movement was possible during the daylight. Many of the men in the firing-line had been on duty for nearly a hundred hours and were utterly worn out both mentally and physically. Such water and food as they had were sent to them at night, for any attempt to cross the open spaces in the daytime the Germans met with fierce bursts of rifle and machine-gun fire. The evacuation of the trenches was, therefore, a most difficult and dangerous operation and that it was carried out with so comparatively small loss speaks volumes for the ability of the officers to whom the direction of the movement was entrusted, as does the successful accomplishment of the retreat from Antwerp into West Flanders along a road which was not only crowded with refugees but was constantly threatened by the enemy. The chief danger was, of course, that the Germans would cross the river at Termonde in force and thus cut off the line of retreat towards the coast, forcing the whole Belgian army and the British contingent across the frontier of Holland. To the Belgian cavalry and carabineer cyclists and to the armoured cars was given the task of averting this catastrophe, and it is due to them that the Germans were held back for a sufficient time to enable practically the whole of the forces evacuating Antwerp to escape. That a large proportion of the British Naval Reserve divisions were pushed across the frontier and interned was not due to any fault of the Belgians, but, in some cases at least, to their officer's misconception of the attitude of Holland. Just as I was leaving Doel on my second trip up the river, a steamer loaded to the guards with British naval reservists swung in to the wharf, but, to my surprise, the men did not start to disembark. Upon inquiring of some one where they were bound for I was told that they were going to continue down the Scheldt to Terneuzen. Thereupon I ordered the launch to run alongside and clambered aboard the steamer.

"I understand," said I, addressing a group of officers who seemed to be as much in authority as anyone, "that you are keeping on down the river to Terneuzen? That is not true, is it?"

They looked at me as though I had walked into their club in Pall Mall and had spoken to them without an introduction.

"It is," said one of them coldly. "What about it?"

"Oh, nothing much," said I, "except that three miles down this river you'll be in Dutch territorial waters, whereupon you will all be arrested and held as prisoners until the end of the war. It's really none of my business, I know, but I feel that I ought to warn you."

"How very extraordinary," remarked one of them, screwing a monocle into his eye. "We're not at war with Holland are we? So why should the bally Dutchmen want to trouble us?"

There was no use arguing with them, so I dropped down the ladder into the launch and gave the signal for full steam ahead. As I looked back I saw the steamer cast off from the wharf and, swinging slowly out into the river, point her nose down-stream toward Holland.

The retreat from Antwerp

On Friday morning, October 9, General de Guise, the military governor of Antwerp, ordered the destruction of the pontoon-bridge across the Scheldt, which was now the sole avenue of retreat from the city. The mines which were exploded beneath it did more damage to the buildings along the waterfront than to the bridge, however, only the middle spans of which were destroyed. When the last of the retreating Belgians came pouring down to the waterfront a few hours later to find their only avenue of escape gone, for a time scenes of the wildest confusion ensued, the men frantically crowding aboard such vessels as remained at the wharves or opening fire on those which were already in midstream and refused to return in answer to their summons. I wish to emphasise the fact, however, that these were but isolated incidents; that these men were exhausted in mind and body from many days of fighting against hopeless odds; and that, as a whole, the Belgian troops bore themselves, in this desperate and trying situation, with a courage and coolness deserving of the highest admiration. I have heard it said in England that the British Naval Division was sent to Antwerp "to stiffen the Belgians." That may have been the intention, the coming of the English certainly relieved some and comforted others in the trenches. But in truth the

Belgians needed no stiffening. They did everything that any other troops could have done under the same circumstances--and more. Nor did the men of the Naval Division, as has been frequently asserted in England, cover the Belgian retreat. The last troops to leave the trenches were Belgians, the last shots were fired by Belgians, and the Belgians were the last to cross the river.

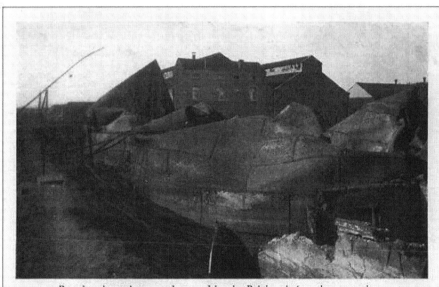

Petrol tanks at Antwerp destroyed by the Belgians before the evacuation

At noon on Friday General de Guise and his staff having taken refuge in Fort St. Philippe, a few miles below Antwerp on the Scheldt, the officer in command of the last line of defence sent word to the burgomaster that his troops could hold out but a short time longer and suggested that the time had arrived for him to go out to the German lines under a flag of truce and secure the best terms possible for the city. As the burgomaster, M. de Vos, accompanied by Deputy Louis Franck, Communal Councillor Ryckmans and the Spanish Consul (it was expected that the American Consul-General would be one of the parlementaires, but it was learned that he had left the day before for Ghent) went out of the city by one gate, half a dozen motor-cars filled with German soldiers entered through the Porte de Malines, sped down the broad, tree-shaded boulevards which lead to the centre of the city, and drew up before the Hotel de Ville. In answer to the summons of a young officer in a voluminous grey cloak the door was cautiously opened by a servant in the blue- and-silver livery of the municipality.

"I have a message to deliver to the members of the Communal Council," said the officer politely.

"The councillors are at dinner and cannot be disturbed," was the firm reply. "But if monsieur desires he can sit down and wait for them." So the young officer patiently seated himself on a wooden bench while his men ranged themselves along one side of the hall. After a delay of perhaps twenty minutes the door of the dining-room opened and a councillor appeared, wiping his moustache.

"I understand that you have a message for the Council. Well, what is it?" he demanded pompously.

The young officer clicked his heels together and bowed from the waist.

"The message I am instructed to give you, sir," he said politely, "is that Antwerp is now a German city. You are requested by the general commanding his Imperial Majesty's forces so to inform your townspeople and to assure them that they will not be molested so long as they display no hostility towards our troops."

While this dramatic little scene was being enacted in the historic setting of the Hotel de Ville, the burgomaster, unaware that the enemy was already within the city gates, was conferring with the German commander, who informed him that if the outlying forts were immediately surrendered no money indemnity would be demanded from the city, though all merchandise found in its warehouses would be confiscated.

The first troops to enter were a few score cyclists, who advanced cautiously from street to street and from square to square until they formed a network of scouts extending over the entire city. After them, at the quick-step, came a brigade of infantry and hard on the heels of the infantry clattered half a dozen batteries of horse artillery. These passed through the city to the waterfront at a spanking trot, unlimbered on the quays and opened fire with shrapnel on the retreating Belgians, who had already reached the opposite side of the river. Meanwhile a company of infantry started at the double across the pontoon-bridge, evidently unaware that its middle spans had been destroyed. Without an instant's hesitation two soldiers threw off their knapsacks, plunged into the river, swam across the gap, clambered up on to the other portion of the bridge and, in spite of a heavy fire from the fort at the Tete de Flandre, dashed forward to reconnoitre. That is the sort of deed that wins the Iron Cross. Within little more than an hour after reaching the waterfront the Germans had brought up their engineers, the bridge had been repaired, the fire from Fort St. Anne had been silenced, and their troops were pouring across the river in a steady stream in pursuit of the Belgians. The grumble of field-guns, which continued throughout the night, told us that they had overtaken the Belgian rearguard.

What the bombardment did to Antwerp. The scene in the Marché aux Souliers, with the Hôtel St. Antoine in the distance

Though the bombardment ended early on Friday afternoon, Friday night was by no means lacking in horrors, for early in the evening fires, which owed their origin to shells, broke out in a dozen parts of the city. The most serious one by far was in the narrow, winding thoroughfare known as the Marche aux Souliers, which runs from the Place Verte to the Place de Meir. By eight o'clock the entire western side of this street was a sheet of flame. The only spectators were groups of German soldiers, who watched the threatened destruction of the city with complete indifference, and several companies of firemen who had turned out, I suppose, from force of training, but who stood helplessly beside their empty hose lines, for there was no water. I firmly believe that the saving of a large part of Antwerp, including the cathedral, was due to an American resident, Mr. Charles Whithoff, who, recognizing the extreme peril in which the city stood, hurried to the Hotel de Ville and suggested to the German military authorities that they should prevent the spread of flames by dynamiting the adjacent buildings. Acting promptly on this suggestion, a telephone message was sent to Brussels, and four hours later several automobiles loaded with hand grenades came tearing into Antwerp. A squad of soldiers was placed under Mr. Whithoff's orders and, following his directions, they blew up a cordon of buildings and effectually isolated the flames. I shall not soon forget the figure of this young American, in bedroom slippers and smoking jacket, coolly instructing German soldiers in the most approved methods of fire fighting. Nearly a week before the surrender of the city, the municipal waterworks, near Lierre, had been destroyed by shells from the German siege guns, so that when the Germans entered the city the sanitary conditions had become intolerable and an epidemic was impending. So scarce did water become during the last few days of the siege that when, on the evening of the surrender, I succeeded in obtaining a bottle of Apollinaris I debated with myself whether I should use it for washing or drinking. I finally compromised by drinking part of it and washing in the rest.

The Germans were by no means blind to the peril of an epidemic, and, before they had been three hours in occupation of the city their medical corps was at work cleaning and disinfecting. Every contingency, in fact, seemed to have been anticipated and provided for. Every phase of the occupation was characterized by the German passion for method and order. The machinery of the municipal health department was promptly set in motion. The police were ordered to take up their duties as though no change in government had occurred. The train service to Brussels, Holland and Germany restored. Stamps surcharged "Fur Belgien" were put on sale at the post office. The electric lighting system was repaired and on Saturday night, for the first time since the Zeppelin's memorable visit the latter part of August, Antwerp was again ablaze with light. When, immediately after the occupation, I hurried to the American Consulate with the package of keys which I had brought from Ghent, I was somewhat surprised, to put it mildly, to find the consulate closed and to learn from the concierge, who, with his wife, had remained in the building throughout the bombardment, that Consul-General Diederich and his entire staff had left the city on Thursday morning.

I was particularly surprised because I knew that, upon the departure of the British Consul-General, Sir Cecil Hertslet, some days before, the enormous British interests in Antwerp had been confided to American protection. The concierge, who knew me and seemed decidedly relieved to see me, made no objection to opening the consulate and letting me in. While deliberating as to the best method of transmitting the keys which had been entrusted to me to the German military governor without informing him of the embarrassing fact that the American and British interests in the city were without official representation, those Americans and British who had remained in the city during the bombardment began to drop in. Some of them were frightened and all of them were plainly worried, the women in particular, among whom were several British Red Cross nurses, seeming fearful that the soldiers might get out of hand. As there was no one else to look after these people, and as I had formerly been in the consular service myself, and as they said quite frankly that they would feel relieved if I took charge of things, I decided to "sit on the lid," as it were, until the Consul-General's return. In assuming charge of British and American affairs in Antwerp, at the request and with the approval what remained of the Anglo-American colony in that city, I am quite aware that I acted in a manner calculated to scandalize those gentlemen who have been steeped in the ethics of diplomacy. As one youth attached to the American Embassy in London remarked, it was "the damndest piece of impertinence" of which he had ever heard. But he is quite a young gentleman, and has doubtless had more experience in ballrooms than in bombarded cities. I immediately wrote a brief note to the German commander transmitting the keys and informing him that, in the absence of the American Consul-General I had assumed charge of American and British interests in Antwerp, and expected the fullest protection for them, to which I received a prompt and courteous reply assuring me that foreigners would not be molested in any way. In the absence of the consular staff, Thompson volunteered to act as messenger and deliver my message to the German commander. While on his way to the Hotel de Ville, which was being used as staff headquarters, a German infantry regiment passed him in a narrow street. Because he failed to remove his hat to the colours a German officer struck him twice with the flat of his sword, only desisting when Thompson pulled a silk American flag from his pocket. Upon learning of this occurrence I vigorously protested to the military authorities, who offered profuse apologies for the incident and assured me that the officer would be punished if Thompson could identify him. Consul-General Diederich returned to Antwerp on Monday and I left the same day for the nearest telegraph station in Holland.

The whole proceeding was irregular and unauthorized, of course, but for that matter so was the German invasion of Belgium. In any event, it seemed the thing to do and I did it, and, under the same circumstances I should do precisely the same thing over again.

Though a very large force of German troops passed through Antwerp during the whole of Friday night in pursuit of the retreating Belgians, the triumphal entry of the victors did not begin until Saturday afternoon, when sixty thousand men passed in review before the military governor, Admiral von Schroeder, and General von Beseler, who, surrounded by a glittering staff, sat their horses in front of the royal palace. So far as onlookers were concerned, the Germans might as well have marched through the streets of ruined Babylon. Thompson and I, standing in the windows of the American Consulate, were the only spectators in the entire length of the mile- long Place de Meir--which is the Piccadilly of Antwerp--of the great military pageant. The streets were absolutely deserted; every building was dark, every window shuttered; in a thoroughfare which had blossomed with bunting a few days before, not a flag was to be seen. I think that even the Germans were a little awed by the deathly silence that greeted them. As Thompson drily remarked, "It reminds me of a circus that's come to town the day before it's expected."

For five hours that mighty host poured through the canons of brick and stone:

Above the bugle's din, Sweating beneath their haversacks, With rifles bristling on their backs, The dusty men trooped in.

Company after company, regiment after regiment, brigade after brigade swept by until our eyes grew weary with watching the ranks of grey under the slanting lines of steel. As they marched they sang, the high buildings along the Place de Meir and the Avenue de Keyser echoing to their voices thundering out "Die Wacht Am

Rhein," "Deutschland, Deutschland Uber Alles" and "Ein Feste Burg ist Unser Gott." Though the singing was mechanical, like the faces of the men who sang, the mighty volume of sound, punctuated at regular intervals by the shrill music of the fifes and the rattle of the drums, and accompanied always by the tramp, tramp, tramp of iron- shod boots, was one of the most impressive things that I have ever heard. Each regiment was headed by its field music and colours, and when darkness fell and the street lights were turned on, the shriek of the fifes and the clamour of the drums and the rhythmic tramp of marching feet reminded me of a torchlight political parade at home.

At the head of the column rode a squadron of gendarmes--the policemen of the army--gorgeous in uniforms of bottle-green and silver and mounted on sleek and shining horses. After them came the infantry: solid columns of grey-clad figures with the silhouettes of the mounted officers rising at intervals above the forest of spike- crowned helmets. After the infantry came the field artillery, the big guns rattling and rumbling over the cobblestones, the cannoneers sitting with folded arms and heels drawn in, and wooden faces, like servants on the box of a carriage. These were the same guns that had been in almost constant action for the preceding fortnight and that for forty hours had poured death and destruction into the city, yet both men and horses were in the very pink of condition, as keen as razors, and as hard as nails; the blankets, the buckets, the knapsacks, the intrenching tools were all strapped in their appointed places, and the brown leather harness was polished like a lady's tan shoes. After the field batteries came the horse artillery and after the horse artillery the pom-poms--each drawn by a pair of sturdy draught horses driven with web reins by a soldier sitting on the limber--and after the pom-poms an interminable line of machine- guns, until one wondered where Krupp's found the time and the steel to make them all. Then, heralded by a blare of trumpets and a crash of kettledrums, came the cavalry; cuirassiers with their steel helmets and breastplates covered with grey linen, hussars in befrogged grey jackets and fur busbies, also linen-covered, and finally the Uhlans, riding amid a forest of lances under a cloud of fluttering pennons. But this was not all, nor nearly all, for after the Uhlans came the sailors of the naval division, brown-faced, bewhiskered fellows with their round, flat caps tilted rakishly and the roll of the sea in their gait; then the Bavarians in dark blue, the Saxons in light blue, and the Austrians--the same who had handled the big guns so effectively--in uniforms of a beautiful silver grey. Accompanying one of the Bavarian regiments was a victoria drawn by a fat white horse, with two soldiers on the box. Horse and carriage were decorated with flowers as though for a floral parade at Nice; even the soldiers had flowers pinned to their caps and nosegays stuck in their tunics. The carriage was evidently a sort of triumphal chariot dedicated to the celebration of the victory, for it was loaded with hampers of champagne and violins!

The army which captured Antwerp was, first, last and all the time, a fighting army. There was not a Landsturm or a Landwehr regiment in it. The men were as pink-cheeked as athletes; they marched with the buoyancy of men in perfect health. And yet the human element was lacking; there was none of the pomp and panoply commonly associated with man; these men in grey were merely wheels and cogs and bolts and screws in a great machine--the word which has been used so often of the German army, yet must be repeated, because there is no other--whose only purpose is death. As that great fighting machine swung past, remorseless as a trip-hammer, efficient as a steam-roller, I could not but marvel how the gallant, chivalrous, and heroic but ill-prepared little army of Belgium had held it back so long.

What the German siege guns did to Antwerp. When a 42-centimetre shell struck a building that building crumbled, disintegrated, collapsed

Image 1. Belgian artillery battery in action (1919) [Photograph] At: http://www.gwpda.org/photos/coppermine/displayimage .php?album=search&cat=0&pos=9

14226847R00159

Printed in Great Britain
by Amazon